MARKETING REBELLION

THE MOST HUMAN COMPANY WINS

MARK SCHAEFER

BESTSELLING AUTHOR OF *KNOWN*

Schaefer Marketing Solutions

www.businessesGROW.com

First Edition: February 2019

Publisher is not responsible for websites (or their content) that are not owned by the publisher.

Library of Congress Cataloging-in-Publication Data

Schaefer, Mark W.

Marketing Rebellion: The Most Human Company Wins.

Mark W. Schaefer - 1st ed.

ISBN-13: 978-0-578-41986-2

To all the marketing warriors, creators, starters, and rebels who love the world of business and have the courage to make it better.

OTHER BOOKS BY MARK W. SCHAEFER

The Tao of Twitter, Changing Your Life and Your Business One Tweet at a Time

Return On Influence, The Power of Influencer Marketing

Born to Blog (with Stanford Smith)

Social Media Explained

The Content Code, Six Essential Strategies to Ignite Your Content, Your Marketing, and Your Business

KNOWN, The Handbook to Build and Unleash Your Personal Brand in the Digital Age

CONTENTS

THE REBELLION AT THE DOORSTEP

Writing this book was … alarming.

A few years ago, I formulated an uncomfortable hypothesis: Marketers were becoming increasingly ineffective because they weren't keeping up with vast changes in the consumer world. There seemed to be a gap between the rapid pulse of the present culture and what my friends in marketing, advertising, and PR were delivering.

So I dove in. And after two years of research, I can assure you that it's not merely a "gap."

It's a freaking revolution.

When I immersed myself in the latest research, I discovered developments and trends that overturned my view of what it means to be a marketer. Almost everything

I've learned and believed for 30 years in business is being renegotiated ... or toppled.

The truth was so disturbing, so unexpected, and so challenging that I wondered what would happen if I started to write about it. I had a feeling that this would be a very loud wake-up call.

Consumers are in control. The sales funnel is gone. Advertising is dying. Great marketing may anger people. Loyalty is a myth. The traditional CMO role is a thing of the past. Technology may be the enemy. Engagement doesn't matter. Our customers are the marketing department.

For starters.

As you'll learn in the following pages, these dramatic statements aren't all that surprising. In fact, they're an inevitable part of a consumer counterattack that has been on the rise for the last 100 years. Most of us just weren't paying attention.

As business leaders, we have to meet the challenge and do what we've always done – adjust. This book will show you how, and it will challenge you to think about connecting to customers in new and unfamiliar ways. Trust me when I say that it can be done, it must be done, and you are the one to do it.

Welcome to The Marketing Rebellion.

GROUND RULES

If you want to appear smart to your friends, here's the essential answer to every marketing question: "It depends."

I'm not being cutesy. (That comes later.) This is a serious commentary.

There's no one-size-fits-all marketing solution for every company and every industry. What I'm offering you in this book is a general, high-level perspective on new business realities, distilled from reliable research and expert opinions. There are always exceptions and outliers, though.

So, I'm never going to tell you what to do … or not to do. This book is a map pointing to exciting new marketing destinations, but you'll have to make your own decisions about the best paths for your own unique business situation and how you'll reach those destinations.

AND OH, BY THE WAY. THERE ARE GIFTS.

Did I tell you about the prizes? I didn't?

Hidden in the chapters I've featured several valuable, free surprises. They're a reward for making it through each phase of the book … my way of thanking you and encouraging your new marketing journey.

So let's start with gift number one. For my last book, KNOWN, I created an accompanying workbook that was a big hit. It's available on Amazon and outsells many of my other books. For this book, I've also created a workbook and I'm giving it away. All you need to do is visit *www.businessesGROW.com/rebellion* to download it for yourself. There are no strings attached – you don't even have to give me your email address!

The Marketing Rebellion workbook provides bonus content, commentary, and study questions to help guide your marketing plans. It's also a great teaching aid and handout if you want to use this book in corporate workshops and university classes.

In the chapters ahead, you'll also find a handcrafted Marketing Rebellion coloring book, a valuable word of mouth marketing handbook, and other surprises.

I hope you'll visit *www.businessesGROW.com* to find all the fun bonus content I've brought together for you. Go marketers, go.

PART ONE

THE THIRD REBELLION

CHAPTER 1

THE END OF CONTROL

"Whoever is careless with the truth in small matters cannot be trusted with important matters."

—ALBERT EINSTEIN

Like all great stories throughout history, this one begins with soap.

When I was a little boy, the only soap my mother ever used on my precious little bum at bath time was Ivory. The reason was clear: Ivory was among the most advertised brands in the history of television. My mother used Ivory because the repetitive and compelling ads fostered her trust and confidence in the brand.

The Ivory brand started in 1878 when James Norris Gamble, son of the co-founder of Procter & Gamble, purchased a white soap formula to develop a product to compete with high-quality imported soaps popular in the U.S. at the time. The product was first called by the unimaginative yet blandly charming name, White Soap.

Ivory was the first soap to be wrapped in paper and sold in individual bars. In fact, it was the first soap to be "branded" at all – something boring was made to be beautiful, clean, and consistent. It was so pure it floated (the result of a happy accident when a workman left his soap-mixing machine running over his lunch hour, causing more air to be mixed into the batch).

Requests for the floating soap grew so much that in 1882 the company took the unprecedented step of spending $11,000 on its first ad campaign, a radical concept at the time.

Keep in mind that P&G wasn't just mass-producing soap. It was teaching people to depend on goods made by strangers.

It's hard to believe today, but people in the 1880s were accustomed to buying from community stores and had never considered trusting goods made by unknown hands. Before the advent of mass production, mass distribution, and mass media, people in every culture all over the world knew their butchers, bakers, and soap-makers by name. So packaged soap was a mind-blowing innovation.

And it worked. For nearly 150 years, P&G – the largest advertiser in the world – spent continuously and relentlessly on promotions to get their snowy-white soap into our households and keep it there.

Today, the "Ivory Tower" is on the brink of collapse. A brand that had more than 50 percent of the market at one time – and even as high as 20 percent in 1970 – now hovers around 3 percent. Ivory has fallen so far and so fast that P&G has considered washing its hands of its most famous brand.

And it's not just Ivory. Over the last few years, legacy brands like Tide, Pampers, and Crest have also slipped into rapid decline.

It seems impossible that some of the world's best-known products backed by 100 years of advertising and the world's greatest marketing minds are disappearing. Soap isn't being displaced by artificial intelligence. It's not being outsourced to India. It isn't being replaced by solar energy or something else. We still use soap. How can customers' desires be changing in such an astonishing way and so swiftly that these brilliant companies can't keep up?

And then, with one statement from a young woman standing in her bathroom, I understood why this is happening, why it is true, and why the failure of marketing as we know it is inevitable. It's the most powerful business insight I've had in a very long time …

THE HANDS THAT MADE IT

I was visiting some young friends in my hometown of Knoxville, Tennessee, enjoying a lovely summer evening with steaming food and cold refreshments. When I visited their bathroom, I noticed something surprising. This household had a stack of soap from a small, local company that included tantalizing varieties like Honey & Oatmeal and Cucumber & Grit. There was even a marijuana-infused soap. (I would have named this "Dope Soap" … but nobody asked me.)

Handcrafted soap is not a cheap or random purchase.

Some of these bars are selling for ten times the cost of a bar of Ivory soap.

I was intrigued. Why would this young married couple on a budget be turning their backs on famous brands and products that had been built by some of the world's greatest companies?

So, I asked my young host, "Ivory soap has been marketing to you for your entire life. Why did you buy this local soap instead of Ivory, or Dial, or Dove? *Why do you love this brand?*"

She thought for a moment and said, "I'm not sure I would say I love this brand. But I love the hands that made it."

In this simple statement, she articulated such a profound idea and a source of the cataclysmic shift forcing us to rethink what it means to be a business, a brand, and a marketer today.

She went on to tell the story of this local soap company and its founders:

"I've met the owners, and they're awesome people," she said. "They make a product with a purpose. They're committed to building a healthy and sustainable business in our hometown. They care for the environment, and they're using natural, locally-sourced ingredients. They want to build a business based on integrity, and they treat their employees really well. I know that because I've met them, too. That's important to me. They're involved in our community, and I see them at our local Maker Movement events. The soap company owners want to make this a nicer place to live, like I do. These are people I can believe in, and I want to support them, no matter what they sell, really."

I asked her if she had ever seen an ad for this soap.

"No. In fact, I can't remember the last time I saw an ad ... *for anything.*"

I think if you told this story to a Proctor & Gamble marketer from 1970, she would think you just fell out of the sky. My young friend is saying that advertising doesn't matter to her. In fact, she's immune to it. She paid ten times the price of a bar of Ivory soap because she believed in the vision of the founder. To her, that's more meaningful than the soap's price, product, placement, or promotion – the classic "Four Ps" of marketing. What the heck is going on here?

This is just one story, but throughout this book you're going to read many others like it that point to a shift that is nothing short of a consumer-driven revolution.

The fact is, this revolt has been brewing for more than 100 years. We're at the beginning of the third, and (perhaps) final, consumer rebellion. But before we unearth this trend and its astonishing implications for you and your business, let's examine how we arrived at this place, starting with Snake Oil and the Elixir of Life.

THE FIRST REBELLION: THE END OF LIES[1]

Today, we take advertising for granted. It bubbles around us in our daily routines, subsidizing a substantial portion of our online lifestyle.

What was the first ad? I had a chance to visit the ancient Roman city of Ephesus, and I observed what may be a likely candidate. Along a white marble road in the excavated city, you can clearly see a brick with an outline of a human foot and a small heart to the left of it. Historians tell us it meant, "Keep walking to the left to find the brothels!"

Roman brothels aside, advertising and marketing as we know them are modern inventions that became a reliable form of revenue to the newspaper industry in the 1830s.

From the beginning, successful advertising meant drawing attention to extraordinary and meaningful promises. But when *everyone* is creating extraordinary promises, the race will naturally run to the bottom, and attention will gravitate to the most lurid and outrageous alternatives. In fact, those alternatives turn into outright lies. Marketers (a term being used by the 1880s) learned that the public was not discerning or even rational and could be convinced to surrender their hard-earned dollars for products that seemed magical.

Clark Stanley's Snake Oil Liniment promised "A Wonderful, Pain-Destroying Compound to Cure Lameness, Rheumatism, Toothaches, and Sprains." Advertising for The Elixir of Life claimed it would cure any disease known to the human body and boldly promised long, and perhaps eternal, life.

By the turn of the century, the advertising industry was generating revenues equivalent to $2 billion. The industry pioneers who settled in New York City were becoming some of the richest people in the country. Their wealth was built on brazen deception, but it escaped scrutiny because there was no regulatory agency like the FDA or FTC at the time. And the press couldn't call out false product claims for fear of losing their single greatest source of revenue.

That changed in 1905 when a brave editor of *Collier's Weekly* magazine commissioned an investigative reporter and a chemistry lab to shine a light on the unethical claims fueling the ad industry. A few months later, the magazine published "The Great American Fraud," an 11-article series revealing dangerous ingredients in these potions that could result in addictions and even death in lab animals.

In one day, "Snake Oil" transformed from a seemingly miraculous cure-all to a catch phrase that meant "fraud," and that connection persists in America today.

The first consumer rebellion against marketing had begun.

The magazine's shocking revelations resulted in a public outcry for reform. Citizen groups and crusading physicians pushed for legislation to impose labeling rules and guidelines for advertising. President Theodore Roosevelt added to the assault by praising the investigative journalism and promising to deliver a long-debated national Food and Drug Act. The proposal ran into fierce opposition from advertising industry lobbyists, but a watered-down version passed thanks to the relentless public pressure.

The advertising business was disgraced and in crisis.

But the first World War brought unexpected benefits. The government contracted with these new advertising agencies to develop propaganda to support the war effort. The ad industry began to redeem itself through patriotic efforts, and the post-war economic boom launched an advertising spending spree in America and Europe.

As the 1920s closed, advertising had become a major part of the economy, representing 3 percent of the U.S. gross domestic product. By 1930, ad spending had increased by a factor of ten over pre-war levels.

Advertising was evolving to become more scientific, more professional, and very profitable. Agencies scaled through an accumulation of expertise and buying power. Ad campaigns for national products like Ivory Soap were unending and ubiquitous.

But once again, intense competition forced advertising claims into a race to the bottom. Orange juice, milk, and toothpaste were marketed with wild health claims unsubstantiated by science. Cigarettes were positioned as healthful and soothing to the throat. The manufacturer of Vrilium said that a two-inch-long tube contained "healing radioactive alien rays" called vril that could "cure any disease you have." In reality, it was a brass cylinder filled with a potent horse laxative.

As consumerism grew, new products promised to cure ailments and solve problems that had never existed before.

Agencies developed sophisticated psychological testing aimed at fanning subconscious anxieties (bad breath makes you unpopular!). Advertising became an industry of lies once more, inventing public fears for profit.

It was about to be shocked into reality again.

Incensed by the industry's manipulation of the American public, two journalists published *Your Money's Worth: A Study in the Waste of the Consumer's Dollar*. The book exposed the deceptive ad industry through scientific testing and medical testimony, sparking the final battle in the First Rebellion. The book's popularity enabled the founding of an independent testing lab, the forerunner of what is now Consumer Reports.

The book and the new lab represented the leading edge of a broader consumer movement. The 1930s saw an unrelenting journalistic onslaught against advertising practices, encouraging a growing sense of mistrust in advertising.

Some of the most intense critics came from within the industry, from executives no longer willing to live with the constant deception. Helen Woodward, a prominent advertising copywriter wrote a popular book against the industry lamenting that "The realization came to me with a slow shock that I was nothing, we were nothing." Another ad executive wrote that to succeed in advertising, he had to "empty himself of human qualities."

The outcry resulted in legislative reform that gave new powers to the Federal Trade Commission, which enacted tougher rules on false marketing claims and more severe penalties.

The first marketing rebellion – the war against lies – was led by journalists and fulfilled through government regulations.

The second revolution would be far different and even more profound.

THE SECOND REBELLION: END OF SECRETS

When I was a kid, the only way you could view a TV show was by having an antenna on the roof of your house. For some reason I still don't understand, often the reception would be better if a human being stood near the TV. Somehow that funneled the TV rays into your box.

As fate would have it, my young body was perfectly formed for this job. If the TV reception was poor, I would volunteer to stand near the set, sometimes leaning slightly forward with arms spread in a launch position, trying to get the perfect picture. So, I normally stood through every TV show.

For this reason, and others, I hated television as a child. Except Batman, but that's a story for another day.

My point is, these were simpler times. Americans had three television networks and sometimes PBS (Public Broadcasting) beaming through those antennas. We were a captive audience for advertisers, whether we were standing up or sitting down. If you wanted to watch a show, you had to see the ads. Lots and lots of ads. But that was about to change because consumers didn't like the ads. And when consumers fight back against something they don't like, they ultimately win.

The second consumer rebellion was enabled by technology. The first remote control that allowed you to skip ads from your couch was developed by Zenith in 1950. The remote, called Lazy Bones, was connected to the television by a wire. Even at the very dawn of the TV age, consumers were already plotting ways to skip the commercials! Today, the average American household has four remotes, which are misplaced with regularity.

Consumers' power to zap commercials was further enhanced in the 1970s with the invention of the video cassette recorder, or VCR. Recording a show and then zooming through the ads became a family ritual.

Another critical step toward an ad-free world occurred in 1948 when an enterprising inventor developed a rudimentary cable network in Pennsylvania to deliver TV programming to mountainous regions that couldn't receive signals from the city. Coincidentally, at the same time, America's Federal Communications Commission (FCC) issued a freeze on licenses for new television stations, creating demand for more television programming. These two developments set off a wave of investment in city and rural cable systems.

Content providers were already dreaming of ways to use this new system to get viewers to pay for content beyond the three dominant national networks. Would people pay for movies in their homes instead of driving to a theater? Would they pay more to skip the ads? The answer was yes.

The first cable network "super station" was launched in Atlanta by Ted Turner, and in 1975, HBO became the first cable network delivered nationwide by satellite transmission and offering commercial-free programming.

Consumers were gaining more control of their content. The "lies" were gone from ads (for the most part). But most businesses were still run on secrets. The power of information was firmly in the hands of the companies and brands. Industries like automotive, insurance, travel, and real estate made money by keeping details away from consumers. The profit margins were in the secrets.

That was about to change in a thunderous manner.

FALLEN ARCHES

McDonald's is a great example of a company built on advertising ... and secrets.

The legendary story of the iconic burger chain has been told in magazines, books, documentaries, and even a feature film called *The Founder*.

About the time Ray Kroc assumed leadership of the company, McDonald's had just 14 restaurants and sales of $1.2 million. The company's first national advertising campaign ("Look for the Golden Arches") was launched in 1960 as Kroc positioned the company for a trajectory of rapid growth.

Just 10 years later, McDonald's had 1,600 restaurants in all 50 states and about $600 million in sales. Its famous "You Deserve a Break Today" ad from this period is rated by *AdAge* as the best advertising jingle of all-time. The all-American company was even featured on the cover of *Time* magazine. McDonald's was on a roll.

Or a bun.

Never mind.

The 1980s proved to be another high-impact decade for the company, as the fast-food chain – already entrenched in the suburbs – began to focus on urban expansion. Although new burger rivals challenged McDonald's, its sales and market share continued to grow.

By the mid-1990s, McDonald's boasted nearly 20,000 restaurants in 101 countries and was among the biggest advertisers in the world. Their ad spend of nearly $1 billion exceeded the GNP of several small countries. The Golden Arches was the most recognized symbol in the world, even ahead of the cross. McDonald's sold so many Happy Meals that it became the world's largest distributor of toys.

But by 2002, there was no hamburger in paradise. After getting pounded with quarter after quarter of sales and profit declines, the company posted its first loss since becoming a public company. Part of the problem was a widespread concern about the healthfulness of the food. Ugly rumors swirled around McDonald's like gnats in a Minnesota summer. The more it tried swatting them away, the more aggressive the swarm grew as consumers discovered the most significant communication platform in the history of the world – the internet.

False information about the use of cow eyeballs and worms in hamburgers popped up all over the web. Homemade videos purporting to show mistreatment of animals went viral. Rumors churned about the company under-paying employees and serving food that was making America obese. And then there was the most persistent rumor of all: Chicken McNuggets and burgers are made from "pink slime" – meat scraps turned into a paste and treated with an ammonia solution.

The fast-food giant counter-attacked by cutting its aggressive growth plans, launching a back-to-basics food strategy, raising wages for 1.7 million employees, adding healthier menu options, and emphasizing wholesomeness through a catchy new ad slogan: "What we're made of."

The company finally faced their new internet reality by naming its first director of social media, Rick Wion. Rick came from a Chicago-based agency that had handled social media projects for McDonald's since 2006. In an interview, Rick said his marching orders were three-fold: Use social media to build the business, manage customer problems, and establish outreach to target groups of influencers such as mommy bloggers.

The company also planned to use the internet to spread the gospel about their "What we're made of" transformation. It was a simple plan. McDonald's would use social media to drive people to its new commercials highlighting real-life farmers and ranchers who supply its wholesome ingredients.

On the day the spots rolled out, everything seemed calm on the social media scene. After clicking on the hashtag #MeetTheFarmers, people were watching the videos online, and the tweets about the ads seemed to be generally positive.

But that afternoon, Rick moved the conversation to #McDStories to encourage people to keep talking about the farmers. Suddenly, the promotion went sideways. From his eighth-floor office at McDonald's headquarters, Rick watched another kind of story dominate the Twitter feed – horror stories, real or imagined, justified or not, about the restaurant's food, service, atmosphere … and just about everything:

- "Dude, I used to work at McDonald's. The #McDStories I could tell would raise your hair.

- One time I walked into McDonald's and I could smell Type 2 diabetes floating in the air and I threw up.

- These #McDStories never get old, kinda like a box of McDonald's Chicken McNuggets left in the sun for a week

- I lost 50 lbs in 6 months after I quit working and eating at McDonald's

Well … you get the idea. McDonald's had paid for the privilege of having their hashtag promoted on the Twitter homepage, but this was not helping their brand. They ended the campaign within two hours but learned a painful lesson – you can't pull a hashtag! Or, more accurately, a bashtag. The tweets kept coming.

A clever social media idea had become yet another public relations crisis for the company. Mainstream media latched onto the disparaging tweets, and the story – dubbed #McFail – blew up as one of the biggest social media debacles of all time. It was an undeserved honor. Rick told me at the time that less than 2 percent of the tweets were negative, which would be regarded as a huge social media success by most standards. But good news doesn't sell, and the true story of #McFail has unfortunately been lost in the hype.

THE END OF SECRETS

McDonald's had finally learned its lesson. This rebellion had to be taken seriously. There could be no more spin, no more misdirects, and no more secrets. Instead of trying to gloss over real (and imagined) consumer issues about ingredients, animal welfare, and obesity, it would have to come clean. McDonald's realized that the brand image it had fastidiously groomed for decades was now in the hands of its customers and critics.

The company's response was bold. It introduced a new "Our food. Your questions" campaign that encouraged customers to pose any question about the company through Facebook, Twitter, and a dedicated new website (piloted by McDonald's of Canada). The company received – and answered – more than 30,000 questions ranging from conspiracy theories about food additives to the truth about pink slime. One of the most memorable answers was a video of a McDonald's marketing director explaining why a hamburger looks different in advertising than it does in a restaurant. It attracted 10 million views on YouTube.

Eventually the campaign of authentic honesty spread to the U.S. and Australia.

The "new" McDonald's had dramatically adjusted its corporate culture to be congruent with the expectations of its internet-empowered customers.

Even critics were impressed. One said the company had "redefined transparency." Certainly, the program was courageous. But realistically, McDonald's had no choice but to go this route if it was to survive. The Second Rebellion was over, and once again, the consumers had won. There could be no more secrets. Not on the internet.

Today we take the internet for granted, but the impact of the End of Secrets can't be overestimated. Putting information in the hands of consumers thoroughly transformed the process of buying a car, planning a vacation, buying insurance, assessing health and medical conditions, purchasing a home, and investing in stocks, to name just a few common consumer transactions.

I worked in corporate marketing during this tech-led rebellion, and from a business perspective, it was terrifying. Almost every marketing function, strategy, and tactic was disrupted. The tech was changing our business so completely and so quickly that we didn't know what was going to happen next.

When we lost our business secrets to the internet, we all went through the stages of marketing grief: shock, denial, anger, depression, and blaming the lawyers. Eventually there was acceptance and a determination to figure out this new world.

If you remember the feeling of chaos in those days like I do, well, the fun is just beginning. The final rebellion has begun, and this time, the consumers have taken charge – and they're playing for keeps.

THE THIRD REBELLION: THE END OF CONTROL

Let's go back to the soap story for a moment. What does it reveal about the inevitable next rebellion? Here are five clues:

1. My young friend built an emotional attachment to the humans behind the product more than to the product itself. The soapmakers helped her believe in their vision and their cause without ever actually *selling* anything. Who is the human we can believe in at Ivory?

2. My young friend is immune to traditional advertising, even when an iconic product like Ivory soap has been promoted heavily for more than 100 years. She explained to me that she streams her television shows, listens to ad-free satellite radio and podcasts, and has an ad-blocker on her phone and computer. She literally sees no ads.

3. There is no "marketing" for this local product in any traditional sense. My friend bought the soap because she could see a tangible benefit in her community. And she paid a lot more for it compared to established brands. The value of the *purpose* behind the company and alignment with her personal values outweigh any need to economize and buy the safer choice of Ivory soap.

4. She told this story in such a compelling way that it made *me* want to buy the soap, too. The power of word-of-mouth referrals and a social media-fueled supply chain levels the playing field, eliminating the historical barriers of owning shelf space at mass retailers or contracting with gigantic New York ad agencies. A story that is meaningful, believable, and relevant can define the brand. The company's story is so authentic that it's passionately carried forward by my young friend. *The customers are now the marketers.*

5. There was no sales funnel, at least not like the one in your company PowerPoint deck. There was no "customer journey" to dissect other than the one that my friend chose for herself. How do you market to a person who is seemingly unreachable? In fact, proudly unreachable.

In this example, we see our foundations of command-and-control marketing collapsing before our eyes like an avalanche.

There are no more lies.

There are no more secrets.

There is no more control.

For more than a century we've built our greatest brands like Ivory through an accumulation of advertising impressions. But to survive this final rebellion, companies and brands must be built through an accumulation of *human impressions*.

That is the only thing we trust. That is the only thing that matters.

This is not a new idea. In fact, it's the oldest idea in marketing. Deep down, we've always known that business is about emotion and relationships. We buy from those we know, like, and trust. We just forgot about that because advertising, PR, and even social media blasts are incredibly cost-effective and have worked so darn well.

Or, at least they used to …

THE WORLD WE THINK WE KNOW VS. THE WORLD THAT IS

As CEO of Buyer Persona Institute, Adele Revella has overseen thousands of customer interviews spanning dozens of industries, and she told me there is one, pervasive aspect of almost every buyer's journey: "Almost no one can recall any marketing engagement that influenced their decision," she said.

"I know that sounds terrifying and I don't like communicating bad news. But I cringe every time I see a graphic depicting an elaborate buyer's journey that is utterly unrelated to anything a real buyer has ever told us. It's clear that sales are occurring from activities outside our traditional marketing programs -- peer recommendations, reviews, and word of mouth referrals from trusted colleagues. Although we occasionally hear mentions of touchpoints such as webinars, whitepapers, or case studies, most buyers tell us that vendor content can't be trusted.

"As a career sales and marketing professional, I feel like we're living in an echo chamber that continually reinforces our own ideas and methods. We're reading content and listening to our peers, all of whom are invested in defining, clarifying, and increasing the importance of our own marketing when the true customer journey is owned by the customer."

The once-predictable sales funnel has become a snarled maze.

Landmark research from McKinsey[2] revealed just how dramatically consumer behavior has flipped the world of marketing in this Third Rebellion. The company found that on average, two-thirds of the touchpoints during the evaluation phase of a purchase involve *human-driven marketing activities* like internet reviews, social media conversations, and word-of-mouth recommendations from friends, family, and online experts.

THE MARKETING THAT WORKS

Let that sink in for a moment. *Two-thirds of your marketing ... is not your marketing.*

This momentous change in consumer behavior means that businesses must pivot beyond push-style marketing communications and somehow learn to influence the unfamiliar two-thirds of the pie that are consumer-driven.

Here's the kicker: That seminal McKinsey article *was published in 2009.* We've known about this consumer revolution for a long time, and yet nearly every marketing organization I work with is still operating with the traditional playbook of TV ads, lead nurturing, and targeted messaging delivered to ideal personas dreamed up by an ad agency.

Ten years later, McKinsey revisited this famous report, and after studying more than 125,000 consumer decision journeys across 350 brands in 30 industries, they concluded that loyalty is more elusive than ever. Ninety percent of the categories showed *no customer loyalty.*[3]

The evidence is there, and it has to be showing up in our results, but marketers are disregarding the revolution brewing right under their noses.

When I wrote about these epic changes on a LinkedIn post, one senior executive violently disagreed with me and responded "Marketing is marketing. As long as we have ads and we can control the message, we're going to be OK."

You see, many marketing, advertising, and PR professionals are asleep, and they don't even know they're asleep ... like this fellow.

I get it.

Rebellions are hard.

Rebellions are inconvenient when your career has been going so splendidly.

Rebellions don't fit into the current social media dashboard.

So, here's the deal. I'm offering you the red pill.

Remember the famous scene in *The Matrix* movie where rebel leader Morpheus holds out his hands and offers Neo two pills? It goes like this:

"You take the **blue pill** – the story ends, you wake up in your bed and believe whatever you want to believe. You take the **red pill** – you stay in Wonderland, and I show you how deep the rabbit hole goes. Remember: All I'm offering is the truth. Nothing more."

This book is your red pill.

Put it down … and you can probably maintain some blue-pill life of blissful ignorance as you try to "control your marketing messaging" until you retire or get fired.

But take the red pill and join this rebellion … well, you're in for a wild ride, my friend. The truth is strange, the truth may make you squirm, but the truth is your freedom.

We're moving inexorably toward a subscription-driven, human-driven, emotion-driven, ad-free, funnel-free, big brand loyalty-free world … and the alarm bells are ringing.

Even if our customers stop watching Netflix and Amazon (where there are no ads), stop listening to their music on iTunes and Spotify (where there are no ads), stop reading their ad-free news subscription, and stop using the ad-blocker on their mobile device long enough to even see your ad, they don't believe it any way. Nearly 80 percent of consumers don't trust corporate advertising in any form, and the percentage is even higher for younger customers. This is a number that has been in decline for at least a decade.

You'll discover in the following chapters that the very foundations of traditional marketing – our channels, strategies, agency relationships, and even the promise of customer loyalty for a job well done – are disintegrating.

The customers are in control.

The customers are the marketing department.

The customers will eventually win the Third Rebellion, as they've won every battle for the last 100 years. I can't change those facts. But maybe I can change you.

We must prepare, embrace the chaos of our age, and discover an entirely new way to connect to our customers.

Which is why we're here.

CHAPTER 2

ALL THINGS HUMAN

"Marketing is going through an existential crisis."

—ASHLEY FRIEDLEIN, ECONSULTANCY

I've written seven books and four updated editions over the last 10 years. I've never had a plan or strategy to write books. I simply write books when I'm puzzled by a trend I don't understand. This book started with an observation: *My marketing friends are stuck.*

This is true everywhere, for everyone, and at almost every company I know.

Even the biggest marketing stars at the most famous brands seem to be struggling. Every year, I'm honored to help facilitate an invitation-only meeting of Chief Marketing Officers. It includes some of the biggest names in business, who use this private meeting to engage in honest roundtable discussions about the most-pressing marketing topics of the day.

At the last meeting, we went around the table and each executive named their biggest challenge. One-by-one they all exclaimed, "We're falling so far behind ... *on everything!*"

I almost laughed out loud. These are experienced, deeply respected executives with some of the biggest companies in the world. They have limitless resources, access to the best people, and premier agency partner relationships. And yet they echoed the same desperate sentiment I hear every day from small businesses, nonprofits, universities, and entrepreneurs with little or no budget at all. Things are just not working like they used to.

Here's the problem: Most marketers aren't recognizing the impact of the Third Rebellion. The world is moving ahead – WAY ahead – but they aren't. They *think* they are because they're attending conferences about artificial intelligence, blockchain, marketing automation, content curation systems, social media war rooms, virtual reality, search engine optimization, voice search, and other technologies changing the business landscape.

Of course, there's an important place for all those innovations in our marketing future. But they will matter very little if we overlook the transformation occurring with *our customers* – this consumer rebellion that is rendering our familiar strategies obsolete. Using the sexy new tech won't matter if the strategies behind it are wrong.

And the research shows that, indeed, those strategies are wrong! The findings of a recent study[4] across the U.S.,

U.K., and Australia illustrates how profoundly marketers are misfiring with consumers:

- Businesses think just 13 percent of their marketing messages are unsolicited, while consumers feel 85 percent of the messages they receive from businesses are spam.

- Businesses believe 81 percent of their marketing messages are relevant and useful, in contrast with 84 percent of consumers who say these communications are NOT useful at all!

- Businesses say they're slow to respond to consumers about 25 percent of the time, but consumers disagree and contend that businesses are slow 83 percent of the time.

- Businesses believe that 75 percent of their corporate communications are personalized, while consumers feel it is more like 17 percent.

While some variance between marketers and consumers is expected, these numbers show a shocking, overwhelmingly negative divide between a marketer's perception of the job they're doing versus the consumer's reality.

In other words, marketers around the world are telling me they're lost, and consumers are saying, "Yes, you're right – you *are* lost."

"Studies show that more than half of the population does not believe marketing claims,"[5] said Avtar Ram Singh, head of strategy for Singapore-based Falcon Agency.

"Marketers are quick to make massive promises in their advertising, talking about how they're premium, they value transparency, they're all about solving problems ... and yet, when it comes to the actual product or service experience, those promises are rarely maintained. It's more than a gap in understanding. It has become an industry debacle. It's one of the most frustrating things to see as a marketer."

What's going on here? Why has marketing become so confused and ineffective? Why are we out of touch with the revolution showing up so plainly in our marketing research and dashboards?

As I talk to my marketing colleagues around the world, there appear to be four dynamics keeping them "stuck" and falling behind:

1. CRUSHING TECHNOLOGICAL CHANGE

A feeling of helplessness about the pace of change leads to uncertainty about direction, effectiveness, and even personal relevance as a leader. I've been in marketing for more than 30 years, and I contend the field has changed more in the last two years than in the last 20.

Marketing consultant Paul Sutton told me, "I advise large companies on digital media. I run a conference. I have a blog and a podcast. I'm quoted in the media as an expert. And yet it honestly scares me to realize how much I *don't* know.

"I look around the world of digital communications, and I'm a deer in the headlights. Artificial intelligence, automation, and all the other technologies impacting us are daunting. I also realize that these things that scare me aren't even on the radar of most other marketers. Being scared is a good sign, I suppose. At least I know what I don't know."

Marketers are also *overwhelmed* by data ... customer contact data, website behavioral data, purchase data, and post-purchase experience data. Nearly 60 percent feel they can't keep up with the technology overload, and just 16 percent of all marketing leaders are confident that they have the right tech in place to do their job.[6]

And the greatest changes are yet to come. Google co-founder Sergey Brin said that the emerging boom in artificial intelligence is creating a "technology renaissance" that will drive rates of unprecedented change.[7] "The new spring in artificial intelligence is the most significant development in my lifetime," he said. "*Every month,* there are stunning new applications and transformative new techniques. Such powerful tools bring with them new questions and responsibilities."

Here's a chilling thought: Today is the slowest day of technological change you will ever witness! The pace is relentless, accelerating, and overwhelming. We're not just dealing with FOMO (fear of missing out). We're dealing with a fear of being left behind.

2. OVER-RELIANCE ON TECHNOLOGY AND AUTOMATION

Too often today, marketing has become a glorified IT department. Customer-facing decisions are being made by statisticians and data scientists in ways that may increase efficiency – and perhaps even sales leads – but drive us away from the heart of our customers. It's not unusual for a CMO to have a bigger tech budget than the IT department, but how many marketing leaders truly have the skills to manage that?

Last year, the lease was expiring on my BMW automobile. I received four automated emails from four different people at the local dealership offering special deals to entice me into a new lease. I asked the dealership which of these confusing offers I should pay attention to and was told by somebody with the title of "internet manager" to follow the communications from my sales rep, Jason.

I emailed Jason and received a confirmation that he would meet me at 9 a.m. on a Tuesday morning, literally the only day I had available that month. When I arrived at the dealership, Jason wasn't in yet and I was told to wait in a lounge. After 30 minutes, I asked about Jason and was told that it was his day off. "How can that be?" I asked. "I received an email from him just last night confirming my visit this morning!"

"Oh, all those messages are automated," the receptionist explained. "Jason doesn't even know they were sent out."

I finally met with a sales manager who had no idea I was coming in that day and had never seen the special lease offer

I had printed out. Even worse, the specific car I was promised was not even in stock. By this time, I was agitated. This over-automated marketing process had wasted my time and raised my frustration level.

"Why wouldn't a salesperson manage their own email?" I asked the manager. "How many appointments could they possibly have in a day?"

"Probably two or less," he admitted.

This is an example of marketing automation that is out of whack. By looking for a marketing "easy button," my local BMW dealership turned an eager and devoted customer into an angry one. (As it turned out, this was just the beginning of a dreadful customer experience.)

Over-reliance on technology has made us forget that those who are buying from us are *people,* not segmented data points on a spreadsheet. The promise of technology is intoxicating, but it can make us lazy marketers who can't see that the customers are now in control.

3. ORGANIZATIONAL PARALYSIS

I've been working with a Fortune 100 company that wisely formed a department in 2010 to create content suitable for the company's numerous social media sites.

Day in and day out for all those years, the employees have been churning out the same bland, stock-photo content for Facebook, Instagram, and Twitter. Meanwhile, employees at the company franchises complain that none of it works anymore. Nobody in the corporate office has bothered to "look up" to see if they're still relevant. They were put there to do a job, and they do it – even if it doesn't work.

They don't see the rebellion because they're holed up in a cubicle.

I see this pattern *everywhere!*

Many of us have been conditioned – and even rewarded – to ignore the profound changes staring us right in the face.

Throughout our professional lives, we've attended training classes to learn to "sell, sell, sell" and "always be closing."

We've created wonderful brands based on heritage and the foundational idea that customers want to be loyal to us.

We've received raises and promotions by integrating marketing technology in ways that can increase "reach" at lower costs.

Our marketing teams work very hard to follow "the rules" that have been handed down over decades to please the legal department ... which at many companies is a sign of success in itself!

Becoming locked into marketing tactics like these might be due to outdated agency relationships, organizational resistance, cultural obstinance, lack of skilled leadership, relentless bureaucracy ... or some combination of all these factors.

"Marketers have become very focused on their own specific role in the customer journey," said Olga Andrienko, head of global marketing for SEMrush. "For example, they may be good at optimizing online ads or creating a certain type of content. But they're not looking at the world holistically and seeing consumers accurately. Their mind is blocked by the task of optimizing one channel they take care of."

A statistic that seems to quantify this paralysis comes from Nielsen.[8] They report that in a survey of brands with at least $1 million in annual marketing spending, the most popular method to decide how much to spend on a marketing budget is to tweak the amount spent in the previous year.

You can't keep pace with a consumer revolution by tweaking your way to glory, my friends.

4. THE COMFORT OF MEASUREMENT

Understanding and serving the two-thirds of our marketing being led by our customers means migrating to unfamiliar marketing territory. And with that comes anxiety, especially when our marketing measures move away from well-accepted metrics and department dashboards.

"There is some overlap between traditional marketing and the new customer journey," said Julie Ferrara, assistant department head - business analytics and statistics at the University of Tennessee. "Customers are choosing their own journeys and pulling information from a variety of places, including traditional advertising and business content. So we don't necessarily need to completely abandon what we're doing, but we need to re-think the role of established marketing channels and optimize them for the new consumer environment. Then, businesses should feel better about taking risks on new marketing tactics with less established measurement processes. It's an evolution."

To succeed today, businesses will have to grow comfortable with marketing through experimentation and iteration in the "two-thirds" -- even when the measures are less clear. That will require a mindset shift that I'll cover more fully in Chapter 12.

5. TECH IS CHANGING CONSUMER BEHAVIOR DRAMATICALLY

The three marketing rebellions have ended marketing lies, secrets, and control. The empowering force since the 1950s (and that crude Lazy Bones TV remote!) has been technology. Today, the methods of product discovery, acquisition, and delivery have been revolutionized. Hyper-empowered consumers are less loyal, more informed, and less trusting of companies and brands than at any other time in history.

Technology is also helping us discover more about ourselves.

As our DNA-ingrained human nature intersects with new technology – including mind-bending experiences we could never imagine – we're constantly uncovering new aspects of our latent humanity. Not only are we learning new things about ourselves, but we're also learning how to use technology to *manipulate* those tendencies, for better or for worse. Our view of human behavior will be much different five years from now as the human-machine interface winds together ever more tightly.

The primary reason business leaders are overwhelmed and paralyzed is because they're preoccupied with technology and a fear of being left behind. Instead, they need to be obsessing over the dramatic new customer realities that are making their strategies obsolete. In short, the tail is wagging the dog.

"In our field of marketing, experience is a *burden*," said Olga Andrienko. "In other disciplines, the world hasn't really changed all that much. Take sales, for example. There are certain cold call skills, emotional appeals, sales triggers ... and then you're done. It's been that way for ages. But in marketing, if you're not embracing the rapid changes and constantly refining your vision, you will fail completely. If you were successful in marketing 10 years ago, that does not mean you will be successful now."

In the last chapter, we learned that two-thirds of our marketing is not our marketing – it's being run by the customers. Instead of paying attention to this much bigger piece of the pie (the activities that are really moving the needle), too many marketers are focused on optimizing the status quo and reinvesting in the obsolete yet familiar tactics of the past.

For the last two years, I've obsessed over this problem and worked to develop a framework that could provide business leaders with hope amid this madness. This is an extremely difficult marketing problem. And I LOVE difficult marketing problems!

Finally, a breakthrough in my thinking came from an insight from the richest man in the world. In fact, he may hold our answer.

BE LIKE BEZOS

No industry is experiencing more calamitous disruption than retail. Specifically, Amazon is reinventing commerce, customer experience, and the rules of consumer engagement.

At first glance, Amazon appears to be the poster child for disruptive technology. But in fact, the real innovation is that Jeff Bezos (the company's founder and the world's richest man) is focusing on what's *not being disrupted.*

While innovations in eCommerce, supply chain, and distribution are the parts of the company we observe, if you peer deeply into the heart of the real Bezos strategy, you learn something radically different, as he explained in an interview:[9]

"I very frequently get the question, 'What's going to change in the next 10 years?' And that is a very interesting question," he said. "I almost never get the question: 'What's *not* going to change in the next 10 years?' And I submit to you that this second question is the more important of the two because you can build a business strategy around the things that are stable over time.

"In our retail business, we know that customers want low prices, and I know that's going to be true 10 years from now. They want fast delivery; they want vast selection. It's impossible to imagine a future where a customer comes up to me and says, 'Jeff, I love Amazon; I just wish the prices were a little higher,' or 'I love Amazon; I just wish you'd deliver a little more slowly.' And so we know the energy we put into serving those needs today will still be paying off dividends for our customers 10 years from now.

"When you have something that you know is true over the long term, you can afford to put a lot of energy into it."

Rather than focusing on the latest trends or leveraging emerging technology for new business models, Bezos has a laser-focus on improving what people already know they love and want.

Amazon, the most disruptive company, is built on a handful of constant human desires – low prices, fast delivery, vast selection – not space-age drones and algorithms.

Technology did not create these human needs. It's quite the opposite. Serving these needs *created the technology.*

This seems like an elegant way to approach the world of marketing disruption, too. Instead of feeling dizzy over these continuous technology shifts, why not establish a foundation for business success that's built on the things that we know *won't change* – constant human truths – and then figure out how technology can be made to serve those unwavering needs?

Consumers have been rebelling against our lies, secrets, and control for 100 years because we're not giving them what they want – what they've *always* wanted.

The most automated company isn't going to win. The best technology isn't going to win. The most carefully planned sales funnel isn't going to win.

The most human company will win.

I'm going to show you how.

ALL THINGS HUMAN

I am here today, writing this for you, because of Philip Kotler, a pioneering marketing author and educator, and Jim Ferry, a former boss. The connection between their stories reveals the main insight and my approach for the rest of this book.

I studied journalism as an undergraduate, but late in my college career, I took a few marketing classes where I was introduced to Dr. Kotler's seminal textbook, *Principles of Marketing.* I was entranced.

Entranced by a college textbook? You may be thinking that I was one weird kid. And I was ... but that's a story for another day.

What got me hooked was Dr. Kotler's description of marketing as a blend of psychology, sociology, and anthropology.

Doesn't that sound like the most fascinating combination of ideas? *The practice of marketing is the intersection of all things human.*

I was captivated and considered changing my major, but alas … I was too broke to remain in school for another year, so I took my journalism degree and went to work in corporate communications. But marketing, and Dr. Kotler's book, were never far from my mind.

CUSTOMERS BEFORE TECHNOLOGY

Several years into my career, I was promoted to become the PR manager of my company's largest and most profitable manufacturing location, a plant in Indiana that produced millions of pounds of highly-engineered materials for the packaging industry. It was a glistening city unto itself – 200 acres under one roof – and a proud showcase of the latest manufacturing technology.

When I toured the location for the first time, I was astonished by a colossal construction site within the plant. My company was building a $50 million facility to produce an entirely new product, leveraging a sensational new technology developed in our research lab.

I learned that the product idea came from one of our marketing managers, Jim Ferry. Jim is among the gutsiest and most progressive marketing leaders I've ever known. He obsessed over customer needs and championed millions of dollars in R&D to discover this radical new coating technology that would increase our customers' productivity, quality, and cost-competitiveness.

The company placed a big bet on Jim and his idea. As I looked over the construction site, I marveled at the futuristic facility that hummed under the bright plant lights, towering over me for three stories. It would be ready in a few weeks and employ 200 people in high-paying jobs.

Jim's idea was creating a new profit center for my company, remarkable new value for our customers, and new jobs for our local economy. If that's what marketing was about, I was all in! I simply had to pursue a career in marketing.

I saw how Jim and his team had used technology in the service of our customers' fundamental business objectives. *My company prioritized technology and invested in it because it served a specific customer need.*

Within a year, I was promoted into a business development position in Los Angeles, and I was finally on the road to a marketing career! As luck would have it, I got to work for Jim, helping him commercialize his packaging idea with large consumer product companies on the West Coast.

I was still young and green in the business world, so I readily soaked up Jim's wisdom.

One day I had the bright idea of reselling our scrap into a secondary market. Sometimes the plant workers made mistakes, so instead of re-melting the material, why not sell it to somebody who had less demanding quality requirements?

Jim was patient with me, but firm. "No," he said. "We can never do that. We don't sell scrap. We sell the best product in our business. If the manufacturing folks realize we can sell our scrap, then over time they'll become sloppy. And when they're sloppy, eventually that will impact our customers and their satisfaction. You have a bright idea, but *marketing is the department that must protect the brand and our customers at all costs.* Everything we do has to be aimed at one goal, customer satisfaction ... even if it costs us money in the short run."

It was this steadfast leadership and stubborn defense of our customers that made Jim great and made our company the best in the business. Jim couldn't be swayed by a tech trend or a short-term opportunity to make some cash. Just because he *could* do something that was profitable didn't mean he *would* do it if that meant hurting our customer. He made sure that everything we did – and everything we didn't do – was consistent with our brand promise.

CONSTANT HUMAN TRUTHS

These are some of the lessons that forged the business leader I am today and spawned many of the philosophies behind this book. No matter how our customers and technology change, the idea that "marketing is all things human" is universal and timeless.

I began to think about the widespread problem I was observing today – how marketers are overwhelmed, ineffective, and increasingly mistrusted. In a world where the consumers are in control, is our profession at risk of becoming irrelevant ... or extinct?

No. It doesn't need to be that way.

Somehow, we need to reconnect with these constant human truths and let them drive our strategy in this rebellious time. Lessons from Philip Kotler and Jim Ferry provide a good foundation for a humanistic marketing strategy:

- Marketers need to leverage technology to serve customers, not abuse them.

- Our guiding principles should be based on constant human needs, not on opportunistic technological forces.

- Marketers need to be courageous leaders who apply these ideals consistently, even when others in the organization may not understand or agree.

- Marketers are the protectors of their brands and their customers, even at the expense of short-term prospects for profits.

How do we apply these ideas in the face of the pressures of the business world today? Where do we start?

After hundreds of hours of research and interviews with dozens of thought leaders from marketing agencies, start-ups, and companies like Dell, Pfizer, Adidas, and Google, I discovered the overarching ideas that should drive marketing leadership for the foreseeable future.

Here are the five constant human truths we'll explore together in the next section of the book.

People want to:

- **Feel loved** (Chapter 3: The Evolution of Loyalty): Loyalty isn't dead yet. It's just not coming from your current marketing efforts. (P.S. A hug can change everything.)

- **Belong** (Chapter 4: The Greatest Human Need): You can belong to a church or a sports team. Can you belong to a company? We'll find our answer by observing laptop stickers.

- **Protect self-interests** (Chapter 5: The Artisanal Brand): Research shows that consumers want to see proof of the value you provide to them and their communities. You can no longer be "in" a city. You must be "of" a city.

- **Find meaning** (Chapter 6: Values-Based Marketing): We grew up with the "Four Ps" of marketing, but there may be a fifth one: purpose. What happens when you need to take a political stand to remain competitive?

- **Be respected** (Chapter 7: Consensual Marketing): Consumers will follow you if there's a fair value exchange. But first, we have to understand what that means in a world where technology dominates our strategies. How do we use technology in a way that truly respects our customers?

Dr. Kotler had it right all along. These five truths line up pretty well with what he taught me through his book decades ago. Marketing really is about all things human:

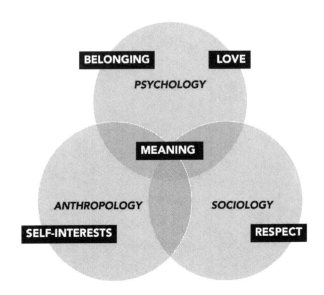

The truth, the answer to our problem, has been in front of us all along ... from a textbook written by a marketing sage 50 years ago.

On the one-hundredth episode of Douglas Burdett's exceptional *Marketing Book* podcast, the legendary Dr. Kotler, now 87 years old, showed that he is very much in tune with the Third Rebellion. He said in his interview:

"What consumers are missing in our high-tech world is high touch. They're missing the satisfaction of real relationships and knowing that other people care.

"If I face a retail clerk who is indifferent to my presence, or I eat at a restaurant where everything is mechanically delivered – even the smiles are mechanical – I don't feel very close to that organization. They're missing *emotion.*

"In the old days, a brand used to be positioned as a perfect solution to a well-understood need. But by claiming that, we ended up disappointing people. That's selling a fantasy. Our message was something like 'this car will make you so attractive to the opposite sex that you have to buy it.' Marketing has been about the over-promise.

"We believed that if we got it sold, then we shouldn't worry about how people feel about it afterward, and that's a mistake. In a hyper-connected world, you can't ignore that the consumer is your most important advocate.

"There's a hunger in our world for real intimacy and experience. Brands need to be more human and authentic. They should stop trying to be perfect. Human-centric brands should treat customers as friends, becoming an integral part of their lifestyle. Brands should be more like humans. Approachable. Likable. Vulnerable."

The wonderful and brilliant man who inspired me to be a marketer when I was 21 years old is still showing me – showing us – the way.

Our customers long for human connection ... and they're in control. We really don't have a choice. We simply must focus on constant human needs and let the strategy follow.

The Third Rebellion is knocking at the door. And the customers are waving big banners that say "Respect Me!"

PART TWO

THE CONSTANT HUMAN TRUTHS

CHAPTER 3

LOVE AND THE END OF LOYALTY

"When mistrust comes in, love goes out."

—IRISH PROVERB

I had been working on an exciting new project and immersed in the latest consumer research when I came across this quote in an Accenture report:

"Our research revealed that consumers are increasingly likely to have a negative reaction to a company's attempt to earn their loyalty."

Wait.

Rewind that tape!

There's a *backlash against loyalty*? But ... as a marketing professional, that's what I've tried to achieve nearly every day of my life for the last 30 years! I *want* my customers to be loyal. *That's my job!*

And yet, the trend is undeniable.

- From McKinsey: "Evidence is emerging that consumer bonds with many brands are slipping. New technologies and greater choice are changing how consumers are thinking and acting across their customer journeys. What surprised us was not only how ephemeral loyalty is, but also how often consumers switched brands once they decided to shop around. Investing too much of your marketing dollars in loyalty is risky."[10]

- From WGSN research: "Our data demonstrates that brand affinity is no longer a direct facilitator to purchase frequency ... retailers can no longer solely depend on their heritage to remain in the consumer shopping basket."[11]

- Rhonda Hiatt of strategy firm Clear reports that 50 percent of consumers do not accept a brand promise at face value, and 32 percent said their distrust of brands is growing.[12]

- ... and this is about to get worse. Gen Z, the youngsters behind Millennials, are even more disloyal and less trusting of brands.[13]

That is downright depressing.

Maybe I want that blue pill after all.

Today, brand loyalty is the business equivalent of going steady, and the breakup seems inevitable.

What comes next? Sure, technology is driving the shop-around movement, one of the most important signs of the rebellion. And there's no way to put that genie back in the bottle. But there's an important clue in that depressing McKinsey report that points to something that might be in our control: *"Consumers are dismissing products if there is no emotional attachment to the brand."*

How can we reclaim that emotional attachment? Let's look at our options.

WHAT'S LOVE GOT TO DO WITH IT?

When it comes to hotel chains, I'm definitely one of those shop-around consumers. Hyatt, Marriott, Hilton ... they're all alike to me. They look the same, they charge the same, they even smell the same. Just find me a hotel close to where I'm speaking or consulting, please.

Except when I visit New Brunswick, NJ, to teach at Rutgers University. Then, I stay at the Hyatt – always – because the lady at the front desk knows me. Terry Olivera is unmistakable with her wide smile and close-cropped silver hair, and when I walk through the front door she exclaims, "Hello Mr. Schaefer!"

Last year, I was struggling through my final business trip of the year. It was December, near Christmas, and I was terribly delayed by a blizzard. My seat on the plane was next to a screaming, sick child, and the trains to New Brunswick were delayed by the bone-chilling weather. As I sloshed my way from the metro station to the hotel, my shoes quickly filled with the gray New Jersey snow-slush-muck (or #SSM as they call it). I was cold, starved, and exhausted.

One look at me stumbling into the hotel lobby and Terry could tell I was having a miserable day. When I returned to my room that night, I had a fruit and cheese plate waiting for me, along with a carafe of wine and a handwritten note from Terry with her wishes for a cheerier day. Because of the delays, I had not had time to eat that evening, so that was dinner, and I was so grateful!

When I checked out the next morning, Terry came out from behind the front desk and hugged me goodbye. I don't know if everybody would consider that politically correct, but I really needed that hug.

In fact, I was so moved by Terry's authentic compassion for me that I wrote a blog post titled "How I Was Hugged by a Brand. Literally." In this world of interchangeable hotel sameness, this singular act of human connection was a welcome relief, and I wanted the world to know about it.

The post went viral, and Hyatt even highlighted it on their corporate website. The next day, Terry got a call at her home encouraging her to come to work right away (and dress up!). When she arrived, the president of Hyatt was there to greet her and thank her for her work. A few months later, she was named Employee of the Year, and Hyatt is now using my blog post as a case study in their new employee training courses. (I didn't even get a free breakfast out of the deal, but that's a story for another day!)

The fact is, we cannot love a logo, a jingle, or a piece of branded content. But we can love a person. That's a clue to regaining our brand standing in a world of loyalty lost.

BRANDS ARE PEOPLE, TOO

Some brands have become a person, or at least have developed a personality, because companies have spent millions of dollars over decades to build irrational attachments to cute clowns and lizards.

- Ronald McDonald is the lovable personification of a hamburger fast-food chain.

- U.S. insurance company GEICO employs an adorable gecko in its ads to make its product memorable.

- I gave a speech in Poland and asked the audience what came to mind when I said "Coca-Cola." Somebody shouted, "polar bears." So even in Poland, people think polar bears drink Coke!

Studies show that consumers form attachments to companies the same way they form attachments with their friends. In their book *The Human Brand,* researchers Chris Malone and Susan T. Fisk write, "Brands are people too. Consider that every company is literally a body (corpus), and as customers, we perceive them as acting with intention and volition, just as we perceive other people."

The Princeton researchers showed that humans judge each other based on two primary factors – warmth and competence – and that they form relationships with brands the same way. In fact, companies and brands were judged so strongly along the lines of warmth and competence that these factors explained *nearly 50 percent* of all purchase intent, loyalty, and likelihood to recommend a brand.

Among the highest-scoring brands in terms of warmth and competence were Johnson & Johnson, Hershey's, and Coca-Cola. Those polar bears are paying off!

Our human mental frameworks perceive brands as stand-ins for people, logos as substitutes for faces, and companies as the equivalent of a social group. Accordingly, we expect to interact with companies in the way we have evolved to interact with real humans.

The bad news is that most of us don't have millions of dollars and decades to turn our brand into a well-known personality that exudes warmth and competency.

The good news is that consumers expect something more authentic and personal today that is within reach of any company with any budget. We can simply show ourselves.

A fan of my blog wrote to me: "I'm a PR professional and I still can't grasp the idea of 'relationships with brands.' Relationships I reserve for people – real people who talk to me. I'm enthusiastic about a handful of brands, but no one representing those brands ever calls me like a human being would. I like these brands – and could even be considered an advocate for them. But not a single person employed by any of these companies has ever 'reached out' to me beyond a push marketing email pitch. Is there such a thing as a brand relationship?"

My friend is correct. It's far easier to be in a relationship with a person than a brand. If it's difficult to get people to love your company, it might be much easier to get them to love your people. No amount of advertising impressions would make me choose Hyatt. I stay at Hyatt because of the *human impressions.* I don't have an emotional connection to a big concrete building next to the Raritan River, but I do have an emotional connection to Terry. We're Facebook friends now.

Aaron Carmichael is a 26-year-old rising marketing star in Atlanta. He told me that to him, the person *is* the brand: "I believe in companies where the values of the founder come through," he said. "My favorite brands stand for something, and I hold them accountable. Just like a friend. If a friend of mine did something that was disrespectful or wronged me in some way, I expect them to make it right."

"I'm not really loyal to a brand. I'm loyal to people."

This is a foundational sentiment of the Third Rebellion. But what are the implications for our companies? Is it possible to create a marketing strategy around human impressions instead of advertising impressions? A new way to think, to be sure ... but it's happening.

SCALING HUMAN IMPRESSIONS

I was working on a digital marketing strategy for a new Adidas business unit. They were a late entrant to a specific sporting goods category, and I had to help them catch up quickly. It was an extremely difficult job – one of the most challenging of my career – because their competitors had a three-year head start and were firmly established in the marketplace.

Serious athletes adore their heroes – wearing their preferred gear, watching their videos, and practicing their moves – and it was no different in this niche. Both Adidas and its competitors had signed contracts with many of these beloved stars to represent their brands. But when I graded each of these contracted athletes on the effectiveness of their social media presence, I found a shocking revelation. All the competitor athletes had high scores – they were doing an exceptional job telling the story of the brand in a human way on Instagram, Snapchat, and YouTube. By comparison, all the Adidas athletes had extremely low scores.

Except one.

An amazing young woman under contract to Adidas, Sasha DiGiulian, had a social media effectiveness score that was through the roof, even higher than the competitor athletes! What was going on here? We determined that all the competitor athletes had been through formal social media and personal brand-building training. Nobody at Adidas had offered this training to their athletes. But Sasha also had a contract with Red Bull, where she learned to cultivate a profound and effective social media presence.

The problem was easily solved. After training sessions and a little follow-up coaching, the Adidas athletes rapidly raised their scores to the level of the competition – and in some cases even exceeded it.

We weren't trying to stylize an athlete to make them conform to a corporate standard. That would have been a disaster. Adidas simply showed them how to be their amazing selves online more effectively and with greater intention, consistency, and reach. That helps everybody.

ENGAGEMENT, NOT ADVOCACY

What if we applied this model to our own companies? Today, having an effective social media presence is a life skill. If more of our employees were trained in that skill (like the Adidas athletes), wouldn't we be better off as a company? Wouldn't employees naturally want to proudly tell our story in the course of their lives, like the athletes?

If customers are less loyal because of a lack of emotional connection (as McKinsey and others have found), would it be possible to establish that bond by encouraging and unleashing the passions of the people who love us most – our employees? Wouldn't that be a logical way to scale those human impressions we need to succeed today?

I want to be clear that the social media effectiveness training I'm suggesting is different than "employee advocacy" programs. Most advocacy efforts are designed to supply employees with company content to distribute to their social networks. Some of the programs are "gamified" with leaderboards and prizes for those who share the most.

I can't find any reliable, independent research on how successful these programs truly are. It's no surprise that the companies who promote employee advocacy initiatives and the software to support them say they're a great success. But employees inside the companies have a different story. A typical response from an employee of a Fortune 100 company:

"The most effective way to represent my company is to just talk about the stuff I'm doing at work. In my old company, I actually sold a lot of our gear just because people were interested in it. Then I joined a company that insisted that employees participate in a gamified employee advocacy program. It's a marketing program that is disconnected from real human relationships and realities – just share company content without any thought to it. Set it and go, just so I can get as many points as I can. The company is focused on reach and impressions, which is driving the wrong behavior. This employee advocacy program is more dangerous to the brand than doing nothing at all."

LinkedIn reports that in an average company, only 3 percent of employees share company-related content, but they're responsible for driving 30 percent of the content's total likes, shares, and comments.

What if we took a different approach that provided true value to the employee by improving their skills and personal brand ... while boosting the employer's brand at the same time?

PERSONAL BRAND/COMPANY BRAND

This is precisely the approach taken by one of my clients, a Silicon Valley tech giant. Their concern was that the innovative heritage and excitement within the company was overshadowed by flashier businesses like Facebook, Google, and Apple. My tech company client was an exciting place to work, but how could they get the word out about it?

They determined that their "cool" could never come from an advertising or PR campaign. It had to come from the people who know them firsthand – their employees. Employees telling the story of their wonderful workplace would be far more effective and believable than any corporate PR effort.

"Personal brand" was coined by management guru Tom Peters in a *Fast Company* article, "The Brand Called You." This was in 1997, as lifestyle branding was beginning to emerge. "All kinds of products," Peters wrote, "are figuring out how to transcend the narrow boundaries of their categories and become a brand surrounded by buzz."

Peters correctly forecasted that human beings would think of themselves as a unique product. The internet had pushed us behind avatars and made us identical – messages stacked in a virtual box – and we would seek ways to break free and differentiate ourselves.

Unfortunately, "personal branding" has become associated with fluffy internet stars and hyperbolic gurus encouraging people to "follow their dream." But finding a unique voice on the web and using it to create the authority, presence, and reputation that creates competitive advantage should be important to every business professional and, increasingly, every corporate brand.

To improve their corporate reputation, my tech company client brought me in to train employee volunteers on the proven personal branding process I established in my book *KNOWN*:

- Accurately identifying your "place" – what you want to be known for
- Defining your space – an uncontested niche to tell your story
- Creating effective content to convey your message
- Building an actionable audience

In the kick-off meeting for this training, we discovered that a young woman had already been blogging about how people were using her employer's technology for social good. Nobody in the company even knew she was doing that!

Consider how much more credible this woman would be in the tech community compared to a television ad on a football game or a post on the company blog. How widely would her message spread if the company supported her, trained her, and helped her inspiring message ignite through the web?

Over time, we trained and nurtured interested employees who wanted to build their own personal brands. Some wanted to do it because they hoped to write a book one day, start a speaking career, or earn a promotion. That's okay. Of course employees were motivated by their own self-interests, but we were sure they would tell positive stories about the company on their own, and they did.

The company even funded personal blog sites, with no strings attached. Not every employee succeeded (it takes time to build a personal brand), but some had wonderful success. One company leader had a post published in the *Harvard Business Review.* Another was invited to give a speech at a prestigious industry conference because of her blogging.

How does that help this B2B brand? How does scaling personal brands sell more stuff?

The company believed, and I do too, that if our employee is appearing in *HBR,* or standing on a stage in front of 1,000 potential customers at a conference – and the competitor isn't – then we will win over time. Our message will be heard. And those accrued human impressions will be more powerful, effective, and long-lasting than any advertisement or press release we could muster.

Another example of a company enlisting its employees to become "known" is American retailer Macy's.[14] Their reason is practical – they were becoming weary of high-paid celebrity endorsers and unreliable (and even unethical) Instagram social influencers.

Macy's enables home-grown influencers by training its own employees to serve as online brand ambassadors through a project called Style Crew. By supporting employee-influencers, the company can more effectively measure reach, monitor legal compliance, and buffer against inappropriate comments or scandalous celebrity behavior.

Candace Bryant, an administrative manager at Macy's corporate office in Cincinnati, has become a bona fide social media star. Warm and charismatic, Bryant gives her coworkers makeovers and tells them they deserve to spend time on themselves. In one self-filmed video, she invites a colleague to share a poignant anecdote about overcoming negative self-scrutiny and developing confidence.

Authentic employee-generated content like this is an important but overlooked option to scale human impressions that lead to a true emotional connection. Let's look at some other alternatives.

A CYCLE OF CONSTANT CONSIDERATION

I was in high-level enterprise sales positions for more than a decade, so when I saw this advice in a research report from a top consulting firm,[15] I nearly fell out of my chair:

*"**Prune spending on closing the sale and loyalty.** Although many marketers emphasize sales incentives and rewards for loyalty, such initiatives are poor at driving consideration and have diminishing returns."*

Just when you thought this rebellion couldn't get any more startling, we're now being told to cut back on something we've believed in for centuries – sales and loyalty efforts!

But when you consider the numbers, you begin to understand why: The research shows that across a broad range of industries, only 13 percent of consumers are loyal to a brand, on average. In some categories like shoes, cosmetics, and financial services, it's even lower than that, and in a precious few industries like automotive and insurance it's higher. But on average, a full 87 percent of consumers shop around, marking a dramatic change from even 10 years ago.

EVAPORATING CUSTOMER LOYALTY

We used to think of our business in terms of a sales funnel. Now, it's best depicted as a cycle of "constant consideration," like a hurricane of human conversations.

The implication of a world with little loyalty is that the focus needs to be on creating constant awareness that leads to consideration for those shop-around customers

– and specifically, relying on our customers to help create that awareness.

We don't own the consumer journey. The consumers do. The new job of marketing is to help customers carry our stories forward into this conversation storm.

Google verified the end of the sales funnel when it analyzed search data across thousands of consumer journeys and found that no two are exactly alike.[16] In fact, even within the same business category, customer journeys take different shapes. People no longer clear a linear path from awareness to consideration to purchase. They're narrowing and broadening their consideration set in unique and unpredictable ways.

I see this in my own small business. Over the past few months, I asked every person who contacted me about speaking at their event how they had found me. Every customer had a different answer! Even in a small business, I'm wondering how I can possibly influence all those touchpoints.

Obviously, I can't. The only thing I know to do is to keep creating those customer conversations that keep me in the consideration set.

STRATEGIES TO WIN IN A WORLD WITHOUT LOYALTY

An interesting way to think about this new cycle of constant consideration is to view "markets as conversations."

This is a keen insight, but I can't claim it as my own. This prescient statement was introduced in a collaborative

1999 blog post called "The Cluetrain Manifesto." The post features 95 theses correctly predicting what I am calling the Third Rebellion. It forecasted that conventional marketing techniques would be rendered obsolete by online consumer conversations.

The post, which later became a beloved, best-selling book, concluded that online conversations about brands are "natural, open, honest, direct, funny, and often shocking. Whether explaining or complaining, joking or serious, the human voice is unmistakably genuine. It can't be faked. Most corporations, on the other hand, only know how to talk in the soothing, humorless monotone of the mission statement, marketing brochure, and your-call-is-important-to-us busy signal. Same old tone, same old lies. No wonder networked markets have no respect for companies unable or unwilling to speak as they do.

"Learning to speak in a human voice is not some trick, nor will corporations convince us they are human with lip service about 'listening to customers.' They will only sound human when they empower real human beings to speak on their behalf."

And we see this happening in our world today. Studies consistently show that content about a brand created by a consumer – in their authentic voice – receives between 600 percent and 700 percent more engagement than content about the same product posted by the company. People trust people.

There is a silver lining to this topsy-turvy new world. In the old days, we would buy mailing lists, assemble email lists, and buy into call lists to double down on a narrow selection of high-potential consumers. But if you follow my advice, a focus on human-generated marketing will open your world to the relevant audience of your audience, many of whom have no previous experience with your products and services.

There are three essential strategies for adjusting to a world with diminished loyalty:

1. Take exceptional care of the 13 percent of your customers who are true loyalists. Give them the tools to be a referral engine for your brand. Stop bombarding consumers who don't want a relationship with endless emails or complex loyalty programs, and lovingly reward your best customers. Do you know them by name?

2. Prioritize marketing efforts that will keep you among the top brands in a consumer's mind when considering a purchase. The brands in the initial consideration set are *more than twice as likely to be purchased* as brands considered later in the decision journey.

3. Focus on consumer-generated marketing such as recommendations, conversations, social media posts, referrals and reviews that occur *after the sale.* These conversations are either creating or destroying the emotional connection to your brand and driving two-thirds of your sales, as the McKinsey study tells us.

How do we tap into that power and join this consideration cycle? Throughout the rest of the book we'll explore those options, including some very specific tactics in Chapter 9. But first, I want to leave you with one of my favorite stories that demonstrates how increasing human impressions can work in almost any business.

LOVE AND THE BORING PRODUCT

I'll close this chapter with inspiration for those of you thinking you sell something boring and not at all sexy. What about scanning electron microscopes? You know the cool, close-up pictures you see in *National Geographic* of scary bug faces, pollen, and other geeky things? A scanning electron microscope is the machine that takes those photos and has many other scientific and medical uses.

On the Schaefer Sexy Scale©, this huge microscope would register as a 3.2, right above printer cartridges. And yet GE's LifeSciences division created an impressive B2B marketing success by featuring its customers as the heroes of the brand story and building an emotional connection bordering on love.

GE asked its scientist customers from around the world to submit their favorite photos from their microscopes for a contest. They received dozens of submissions that were like little pieces of art.

The company then selected the best photos and invited the winners to their headquarters in New York for a celebration. But the scientists were about to be treated to much more than a dinner and a plaque.

As the cameras were rolling, the GE team took the scientists to Times Square and told them to look up. There, in a magnificent electronic display as tall as a building, were their photos! The reaction was amazing. Tears streamed down the faces of the customers as they saw their hard work on display for the world to see. They gasped with astonishment and delight.

This was a lovely story of the common becoming uncommon, the mundane becoming glorious, for just one amazing moment.

Here's why I love this case study so much:

- It was based on human-generated stories, wasn't it? The scientists did the work.

- The project relied on human connections to create an astounding and emotional reaction. The response was so profound that it's still on my mind five years later. GE made its customers shed tears of joy.

- The company is selling a big hunk of technology by celebrating humans through an unforgettable experience. I can imagine what these customers were thinking as they gazed into the night sky: "Somebody *noticed me.*"

- It applied a creative storytelling approach to highlight a potentially boring B2B product. Scientists and engineers are humans, too. Show that humanity. Make that connection.

Did it achieve anything?

The one thing that's missing from this excellent case study is measurement.

Obviously, this was a GE corporate video, so I don't know if this content piece ever sold one microscope, but in the long-term, maybe it achieved loftier goals. The best we can hope for in our marketing today is to connect people to an emotion that results in awareness, trust, conversations, and consideration over time. We aim to connect in a way that propels our story forward through our customers.

GE's customers were *crying with joy.* I guarantee you those business leaders will never forget that evening on Times Square. Heck, I won't forget it, and I wasn't even there. If we could interview those customers today, I know that many of them would use the word "love" to describe the feeling of that moment. They felt like they belonged to a company through a unifying and extraordinary experience. GE may not have been able to measure this effort and connect it to some future microscope sale, but they undoubtedly generated years of stories that will keep them in the consideration cycle.

Mission accomplished.

Stop using your industry as an excuse. Just because you're in banking or finance or engineering doesn't mean you have to be boring. Engineers and bankers love interesting and entertaining content and experiences, too. Nobody will ever choose boring over not-boring, no matter the profession.

My main message is this: Don't fight the rebellion. What should you be doing right now to adjust to a world where *the customers are doing most of our marketing?* What will you do to fight for that emotional connection and constant consideration?

Let's keep going and explore another constant human need that can open opportunities for us in this post-loyalty era: Belonging.

CHAPTER 4

BELONGING: THE GREATEST HUMAN NEED

"The essential dilemma of my life is between my deep desire to belong and my suspicion of belonging."
—JHUMPA LAHIRI

Turns out the Beatles were right, at least according to Harvard University.

In the longest health study in human history, Harvard researchers[17] studied the lives of the same group of people for more than 80 years. Since 1938, they've tracked the intricacies of the lives of this group, documenting aspects of their physical and emotional health, their employment, families, education, economic status, leisure activities, friendships, and dozens of other details.

By looking at human development over a lifespan, the researchers hoped to find trends that would provide insight into what factors ultimately led to a good – and long – life.

After decades of research and millions of dollars, the university discovered that the Beatles had it right all along.

All you need is love.

Long-term contentment didn't come from money, status, or material goods. Those who were happiest and healthiest reported strong interpersonal relationships, while those who were isolated had declines in mental and physical health as they aged. Robert Waldinger, the director of the program, shared that key finding in a popular TED Talk viewed millions of times. His conclusion: "Loneliness kills."

The study put a name to the ultimate human desire. *We need to belong.*

The problem is, increasingly, we don't.

ONLY THE LONELY

On the surface, it seems like there's no reason for anybody to feel alone any more. We've never had more opportunities to be connected. The interwebs are humming and buzzing 24 hours a day. As long as you have wi-fi, human connection is a click away, right?

Wrong.

Using the web as a replacement for human interaction has led to *more* isolation, depression, and major health problems ... not less.

UCLA has surveyed its students and tracked stress levels of incoming freshmen since 1985. Since the first survey, the percentage of freshman reporting that they "felt overwhelmed" more than doubled, from 18 percent in 1985 to a shocking 41 percent in the most recent study. And it's not just a problem in the U.S. A massive study across 237 countries found the same result.[18]

Most scientists agree these numbers are rising due to the unique demands placed on teens by social media and digital technology ... and a commensurate decline in true human connections.

There's a mountain of evidence[19] suggesting that the quality of our relationships has been in steady decline for decades. In the 1980s, 20 percent of Americans said they were often lonely. Now it's 40 percent. Depression rates have increased tenfold since 1960. A study[20] found that an epidemic of loneliness in the workplace is leading to lower job performance and less commitment to the organization, and an individual's loneliness even influences the performance of people around them.

New research showed that more than 9 million people in the U.K. suffer from loneliness, prompting the prime minister to create a new government position – a minister for loneliness.[21]

At this point, you might be wondering, what in the world does this have to do with me and my company? Well, maybe everything.

Let's look at this in purely rational business terms. People have a deep need to belong, but there is a belonging gap in the world, a profound unmet human need, a need that is escalating to crisis proportions.

Is it possible for a company to help people belong?

The answer is yes.

THE BEGINNING OF BELONGING

In the 1960s, Pepsi was in crisis.[22] The American soft drink was being outsold by Coca-Cola at a rate of nearly six to one. Coke was unrivaled in its market, creating ubiquitous advertising convincing their customers that their drink represented everything good and wholesome about American life: Santa Claus, smiling families at the beach, baseball.

In 1963, Pepsi hired a young advertising executive named Alan Pottasch to tackle the problem, perhaps the most daunting marketing challenge of his era. He had to reinvent a product competing against one of the most successful brands of all time, a product that outspent Pepsi at every turn.

Pottasch determined that he couldn't win by talking about the product. He had to talk about the consumer. Tim Wu documented this challenge in his wonderful book, *The Attention Merchants:* "Pottasch conceived of marketing Pepsi without reference to its inherent qualities, focusing instead on an image of the people who bought it, or should be buying it."

For the first time in history, a brand decided to promote a sense of community and belonging instead of the characteristics of a product. Pepsi promoted the idea of an entirely new generation – the Pepsi Generation – that was free from the manipulative messages perpetuated by Coke.

The Pepsi Generation was revolutionary at a historical moment. In the tumultuous 1960s, no generation had ever longed so much to transcend the past –to escape the consumerist mindset and achieve truly independent thought. Pepsi's message was essentially "You belong to us. Stop drinking your parents' drink."

Having a soft drink claim an entire generation was a courageous and bold move. And it worked. The campaign was massively successful, finally establishing Pepsi as a worthy competitor in the soft drink segment.

Those who became a part of the Pepsi Generation weren't searching for a new beverage. They were looking for a new place to belong.

A new kind of marketing had begun.

THE GREATEST COMPANIES ARE FANS OF THEIR FANS

A few years ago, I had an opportunity to work on a year-long project examining the extreme sports market. This was a fascinating experience, and I met some of the craziest people on earth. Perhaps that sounds judgmental or harsh, but there really is no other way to describe them.

These are the outrageous folks who dangle from a 1,000-foot cliff by the fingers of one hand, ride mountain bikes across sheer ice precipices, and happily test themselves against the most extreme weather conditions.

Like I said, crazy.

Perhaps no person better represents this over-the-limits faction than renowned rock climber Alex Honnold. In 2017,

Honnold became the first person to scale the 3,000-foot granite El Capitan precipice in America's Yosemite National Park without using ropes or any other safety gear.

In four hours, Honnold completed what may be the greatest feat of pure rock climbing in the history of the sport. It was a breathtaking human achievement.

It's hard to overstate the physical and mental difficulties of a free solo ascent of that magnitude – an unforgiving vertical expanse stretching more than a half mile into the sky, higher than the world's tallest building. One magazine referred to his accomplishment as "the moon landing" of extreme sports.

Here is how my mere mortal mind works. Yes, I marveled at this accomplishment, but I wondered ... how did Alex explain what he was about to do to his mother?

Extreme sport fanatics are a different breed. They "follow the sun" and often live in the backs of vans to find the best experiences in the most ideal weather. They spend their money on death-defying adventures and often get by on donations from fans or, if they're lucky, a corporate sponsor willing to send some gear their way. By most standards, they are way, way, way outside the boundaries of normal society.

If you appreciate the extreme sport mindset, then you'll marvel at the marketing efforts of outdoor outfitter The North Face and one of the most beautiful and effective videos ever made in the corporate content world.

The video "Question Madness" is easily found on YouTube and has already been viewed more than 8 million times. In less than two minutes, the video shows North Face adventurers bleeding, crying, screaming, and falling from a rock face in exhaustion and anguished despair. "It is weird," Honnold narrates over these images of failure, "having so many people question your motivations ... questioning your sanity."

But as the music swells, new images express triumph, courage, freedom, and exuberant joy.

The fast-paced video flips the word "obsessed" to reveal "devoted."

"Crazy" turns into "calculated."

"Freaks" transforms into "pioneers."

This video creates an astonishing emotional link and justifies an out-of-bounds lifestyle by explaining the unexplainable. Maybe it even helped Alex rationalize his death-defying feat to his mom.

It's North Face's way of saying, "You're okay, you belong."

Specifically, *you belong to us.*

Here's proof of the success of this message. One of the fan comments under the video says, "Now THAT is how you advertise!"

Indeed.

North Face didn't pay to place this "ad" on the Super Bowl or on a popular television sitcom. It didn't promote the two-minute video in an email blast or direct mail campaign. The company posted it on YouTube for their community to find on its own. And yet, it's the best "advertising" we could ever produce, isn't it?

Like any great marketing effort, North Face didn't approach this as a one-off and instead supported the video through a holistic strategy including the establishment of Global Climbing Day, which gives their fans a chance to experience climbing for free at more than 150 locations. The company also brought climbing to underserved communities by setting up free, public climbing walls across the country.

As we move slowly but inexorably toward an ad-free world, *this is the new advertising:* Stories that serve, inspire, and entertain. Meaningful events that demonstrate true caring, compassion, and community involvement. Emotional connection that shows how much we *understand.* This is marketing that helps us belong.

The North Face video conveys hope. And for all the extreme sports "crazies" out there, it builds a sense of pride in belonging to their insane little place in the universe.

Belonging is primal and fundamental to our sense of happiness and well-being. The best companies on earth don't "own" customers. They own a space and help customers belong there.

The greatest companies are fans of their fans.

THE STICKER TEST

Belonging. That is one big, emotionally-charged word.

People might belong to a religious group. Perhaps they have a deep emotional connection to a sports team, a university, or a social cause. But a company? Can you feel true belonging to a company?

Customers are actually telling us that they *want* to belong to our companies. I saw one surprising statistic that 50 percent of heavy social media users thought it was important to receive recognition from friends online. But more than 60 percent said it was important to be recognized by a favorite brand online. Isn't that amazing? The acceptance by a beloved brand is more important than acceptance by a friend!

The signs that people want to belong to a brand are all around us, if you know where to look.

A few years ago, I came across a photo online of a fellow who had tattooed a Nike "swoosh" on both ankles. My first reaction was, "Wow, that must have hurt." But then I realized that this act of self-illustration represents the ultimate marketing success. This runner loved Nike so much, trusted them so much, committed to their ideal so much that he made a corporate logo part of his body forever. In a very public way, he's saying, "This company is not going to let me down. I'm proud to belong to this tribe and what it stands for."

Not everybody is going to go to the pain and expense of tattooing a logo on their body, but there are lots of "virtual tattoos" around that symbolize belonging.

Take a close look at the open laptop cases dotting your local coffee shop or pub. Notice how they're decorated with favorite brands. Pay attention to the bumper stickers on cars and trucks (at least in America). Look for friends wearing branded T-shirts and hats. If somebody loves a company enough to wear their logos on their bodies and stick them on their precious computers and vehicles, I regard that as a tattoo-like marketing achievement.

Getting into the complex psychology of belonging is beyond the scope of this book – perhaps any book – but for the sake of argument, let's say that mindfully attaching logos to body parts, clothes, and cars demonstrates a deep-rooted belief in a brand that is a symbol of belonging.

Here are a few examples of sticker-worthy companies that are tapping into the constant human need to belong.

MOTORCYCLE AS LIFESTYLE

I love zooming through the hills of East Tennessee on my bicycle, and one day I came across a family's mailbox in the shape of the Harley-Davidson logo. Folks, I know a lot of devout Christian people and I have never seen a Jesus mailbox. I could make an argument that the Harley motorcycle brand is a major American religious group.

The devotion to this all-American brand is intense and cultish. We have a dealership near our home that has an entertainment venue attached to it, and every Saturday night, bikers come from far and wide to relax, drink a beer, and listen to live music. They all bring their tricked-out bikes, clad head to toe in their Harley uniforms – branded hats, leather jackets, vests, pants, and boots. About 22 percent of Harley's sales are non-motorcycle accessories and merchandise.

What's going on here? Why are people so loyal to this machine? Let's turn to explanations from actual Harley fans who described their devotion in an online forum:

"Harley is a way of life, not just a motorcycle. Belonging to a group of Harley riders is unlike anything else. Go to the annual rally, and you'll see what I mean."

"HD gives freedom to its riders to customize, and those bikes become conversation pieces. Every rider is a brand ambassador."

"You can't beat that sound. Nothing is more satisfying than the rumble of Harley Davidson right beneath you."

"When someone asks you what type of motorcycle you own, if you say a Harley, their eyes light up, as if that is what they were hoping to hear."

"A big attraction for me is the Harley Owners Group (or, HOG). There's a chapter in most cities. I like meeting friends that like riding. That is where I belong."

"My Harley has this big seat that really babies your butt. After a 12-pack of Mountain Dew and a sack of potatoes, my Harley puts me in heinie heaven. Tell me *any other possession* that makes a fat guy look cool."

"The fact is, for the money, a Harley is crude, uncomfortable, not very fast, and overrated. You can get bikes that do anything a Harley does, and do it better, for a lower cost. Except ... it won't be a Harley. You can't buy cool, but a Harley is a damn good start."

When you buy a Harley, you're not buying a motorcycle. You're buying a sense of belonging to a well-curated community of cool. And speaking of cool ...

HOT LOVE FOR THE COOLEST COOLER

About three years ago I started to notice bumper stickers, T-shirts, and ballcaps that displayed a logo for "YETI." I was somewhat familiar with the Yeti brand of premium ice coolers but could not fathom why any rational person would promote this mundane product. I mean, it's a *cooler!*

And yet brothers Roy and Ryan Seiders pulled off the ultimate entrepreneurial dream of building a product so popular, so durable (it won a test against a grizzly bear), and so conversational that, within a few short years, it became legendary.

The Yeti cooler retails for ten times the price of an ordinary cooler and has millions of passionate fans. For entrepreneurs and product designers, this is the ultimate goal: Turn a household commodity into an object of desire.

With the help of marketing executive Walter Larsen, the startup grew almost entirely through a focus on "human impressions" and word-of-mouth marketing. "I told them the outdoors market is easy and inexpensive to reach," Larsen said, "and that there was a monumental opportunity if they were aggressive."[23]

Larsen helped the brothers create a simple tagline – "Wildly Stronger, Keep Ice Longer" – and focused their marketing on the hunting and fishing audience by hiring influential guides and local fishermen as brand ambassadors. With every cooler shipped, the brothers threw in a Yeti hat and T-shirt to create a conversation around the product. They educated their influencers on the selling points of the product so they could spread the story and defend the high price.

After their initial success, Yeti expanded their human-impression strategy beyond hunting and fishing. They targeted rural feed-and-seed stores because farmers and ranchers work and play outdoors and like to barbecue. Then, they moved their word-of-mouth magic to the snowboarding, camping, and mountain-biking Colorado crowd.

The little company quadrupled its sales in three years.

One analyst commented, "The Yeti story is not about a cooler. It could have been a zillion things, but they've built a community, an operating philosophy, around their passionate commitment to the outdoors. Large corporations would pay anything for this kind of credibility, which is what makes it unobtainable to them."

Predictably, competitors are coming after Yeti as they try to expand into new product lines and international sales. Will they make it? As we learned from Harley-Davidson, a brand that becomes tribal can be enduring.

And oh yes. Yeti just introduced a $1,300 cooler.

IT'S NOT JUST A STORE, IT'S A COMMUNITY

Lululemon has taken the activewear industry by storm. Started in Vancouver, Canada, in 2000 as a single store selling yoga gear, the company has expanded rapidly and has become a beloved global brand. Despite its high prices for products that often sell out quickly (95 percent of their sales are at full price), the retailer has developed an obsessed fanbase.

Although the company is known for its attention to design, durability, fit, and fabric quality, the real point of differentiation is a sense of belonging built through repetitive and constant human impressions. Lululemon has created a space and culture based on the concept "build a better life," and they welcome customers into it.

The Lululemon community spends more, exhibits more brand loyalty, and provides more profitability than almost any group of retail customers on earth.

Let's take a look at how a company like Lululemon helps its customers belong:[24]

1. Conversation through design

Lululemon creates interesting designs that inspire conversations. From tote bags to T-shirts, the company generates provocative images that promote the "sweat every day" lifestyle. Feel-good quotes on store merchandise serve as a form of "social snack" that spurs conversation and reinforces the values of its customers.

2. Employees as conversation-starters

Store employees are encouraged to discuss exercise goals and fitness tips with customers. They feel more like gym buddies than sales associates (in fact, they're instructed to dress like they're going for a workout!). The staff is well-trained to tune in to a customer's fitness passions, talk about them, and provide personalized recommendations.

Most people who work at Lululemon are athletic, so they have shared values with their customers. Each retail location is organized and designed to encourage conversations. Employees have an efficient system to stock and maintain the store, freeing up more time for human interactions with customers.

Nina Gardner, Lululemon's community relations manager said:[25] "Relationships with customers – that's what really sets us apart from being just another retail store that's opening up to sell clothes. Absolutely we sell clothes, but more important, we are building relationships. We are supporting communities."

3. Stores as conversation hubs

To help pay the rent when the company was a startup, Lululemon founder Chip Wilson used his office space as a yoga studio at night. That tradition continues today, and the company's stores still host yoga and fitness events after hours, in essence turning a retail store into a "fitness and conversation hub" that encourages return customer visits.

The company also hosts live, national events and retreats where customers can connect and meet executives and top fitness influencers.

4. Activate community influencers

A year before each new store opens, Lululemon scouts the immediate area to identify influential yoga, running, and fitness instructors willing to become local community ambassadors. In exchange, the ambassadors get discounts on Lululemon clothing and may lead their classes within the stores.

Lindsay Claydon, Director of Brand and Community - Europe, said the elite ambassadors also serve as an R&D lab by contributing to the brand's design process, testing products, and providing feedback on stores and programs.

"Stores choose local ambassadors who are leaders in their respective community and reflect our culture and passion for fitness and health," she said. "This creates more authentic and engaging relationships and supports the brand in building connections with consumers it may not have reached previously."

Lululemon isn't just selling clothing. They're building a community with a shared value of joy through fitness.

THE ACCIDENTAL SUPERSTAR

I've provided examples of how companies of all sizes have made people feel like they belong, but what about a single person?

Pat Flynn is well-known in entrepreneurial circles for his candid, funny, and completely transparent business style. His approach is forged from some hard knocks.

In 2008, Pat was laid off from his dream job with an architectural firm. But he had developed expertise helping people pass professional exams, and on a whim, he started a free website to help people ace their tests. To his amazement, the site received thousands of visitors each day.

Pat was giving away his advice, but people told him it was so good that they would pay for it. He created an eBook, a study guide, a digital book, and started charging for his services. In the first month, he made $7,000, which was a life-changing lesson for the new entrepreneur.

This success led Pat to build another site, SmartPassiveIncome.com, where he blogged about the ups and downs of his entrepreneurial adventures. When he experimented with podcasting, his community really took off.

"The podcast allows for storytelling," he told me, "which is what people relate to. They feel you, they hear your emotion, they hear your voice. Revealing things about my life connected me to my fans. Now we're at this place where we can talk like friends."

I had heard about Pat several years ago, but it wasn't until I saw him speak at a conference that I realized how frenzied his fans were. Like, rock star frenzied. There were lines of people waiting to meet him. This guy has a special sauce. The "entrepreneur advice" space is massively saturated, so how did Pat beat the odds?

"I give people attention," he told me. "Community is just a byproduct of that attention. And the reason I do that is because when I started my company, I did a lot of research into internet marketing, online business, entrepreneurship ... and I never felt like I could connect with anybody. The business leaders were secretive, they wanted me to pay money to get close to them. That just felt kind of creepy.

"I wanted to take a different approach. I'm going to make you feel like I actually care, because I do! I was in their shoes not too long ago. So, I'm going to reply to every single comment on my blog. I'm going to respond to every single message on social media. I'm going to reply to every single e-mail, and I'm going to try to do it within 24 hours.

"I also wanted to be honest with people. I share the failures as well as the wins because to an audience, failures are always more interesting. Everybody makes mistakes, so if you share mistakes, people know you're the real deal.

"When I started my site, I shared the information about running a new business that I couldn't find anywhere else – how many sales I was getting, how many customers, and how much money I made that month. I actually had planned to do it for just a month – it was unheard of to share your income reports online – but I got so much great feedback that I just kept it going.

"Making this group of people feel they belong to something was not intentional at first. But it happened because I gave them attention, and now they're giving each other attention because we have shared interests and values. Because of the internet, it's so easy to have people find you and come onboard. Then the community brings other people they care about onboard."

Pat found that his growing fanbase ignited into something bigger when they had a chance to meet him face-to-face.

"I was at a conference and invited people to come meet with me. A hundred people signed up in a couple of minutes. And another 150 people didn't sign up and tried to crash it because they wanted to be there, too. That showed me how passionate people were about being part of this group. And for a person who just records a podcast from his home office, to see that there are actual human beings who want to be a part of this ... is just mind-boggling.

"There is tremendous value in seeing people face-to-face," he said. "I think it's important – whether you're an individual or a business – to create those moments where people can come together, because they take away experiences. They take away memories. It turns them into superfans.

"A difference between customers and fans is that fans want to be *involved*. When they feel included, they become invested. When they are personally invested, they may also invest with their dollars.

"Bottom line, people want to belong only when they can see something real. I show them where I work. I show them I drive a minivan because I have kids. I shoot video when I'm not feeling well. I do a lot of behind-the-scenes Instagram stories. I use the social channels to be the person I am on my website.

"You may love me, you may hate me, but I'm the same. I'm real. That's our business world today. And you know, it's going to be so difficult for a lot of companies to make that transition."

HOW TO HELP PEOPLE FEEL THEY BELONG

When you help people feel they belong, they'll stick with you in hard times, spend more (even on a cooler!), and spread your story better than any advertising you could buy. It gives you an incredible marketing advantage.

Building a brand that enables a true sense of belonging can be difficult, however.

Here are eight ideas to consider if this seems like an option for your company:[26]

1. A brand community is a business strategy, not just a marketing strategy.

Too often, companies isolate their community-building efforts within the marketing function. That's a mistake. For a brand community to yield maximum benefit, it must be framed as a high-level strategy supporting business-wide goals.

Harley-Davidson is a great example. In the 1980s, management completely reformulated its business model around a brand community philosophy. Beyond just changing its marketing programs, Harley-Davidson retooled every aspect of its organization – from its culture to its operating procedures and organizational design – to drive its community strategy, the "brotherhood" of riders.

I once had an opportunity to be in a sales meeting with top Harley executives. My company had invented a new type of aluminum that resisted dirt and grease. We thought it would be a perfect fit for a motorcycle.

"No," the exec told us. "Our riders love to clean their bikes. That's how they interact with our product. The dirt belongs there."

Nurturing their community wasn't just a marketing strategy to sell stuff. It was a business strategy that was tuned in to the emotional needs of its customers.

2. A brand community exists to serve the people, not the business.

Managers often forget that consumers are real people with many different needs, interests, and responsibilities. A community-based brand builds loyalty not by driving sales transactions but by helping people meet their needs.

How does a company stay tuned in to emerging needs? Futurist Faith Popcorn said, "Look for the signals of tomorrow – step out of your comfort zone, delve into pockets of the culture you usually avoid. Then you connect the dots. Go to underground bars and clubs and offbeat cafes; see what people are eating and saying. Go sound-bathing. Try cryotherapy. And ask yourself, what need is this answering, and how can my business address that need?"[27]

3. Smart companies embrace the conflicts that make communities thrive.

Most companies prefer to avoid conflict. But communities are inherently political, and conflict is the norm. "In" groups need "out" groups against which to define themselves. PlayStation gamers dismiss Xbox. Apple enthusiasts hate Microsoft. Ford truck owners shun Chevy owners. Community is all about rivalries and lines drawn in the sand.

I dive into this idea more in Chapter 6, but taking a stand to bring together a community is one of the few remaining strategies that can create true brand loyalty. Communities become stronger by highlighting, not erasing, the boundaries that define them.

4. Communities can bestow status.

Affiliation with a group can provide a powerful sense of status, and that status can be enhanced by activities and even leadership within the group. Nothing creates advocates more than bestowing status within your community.

Robust communities establish cultural bedrock by enabling everyone to play a valuable role. For example, Pat Flynn mindfully and consistently rewards top contributors and bestows status, which inspires others to contribute.

5. Look them in the eye.

I've written extensively in my other books about how web connections are weak relational links. They're important because they enable potential opportunity, serendipitous connections, and new ideas, but the magic really happens in a community when you bring people together face-to-face.

Turner, an Atlanta-based company that produces popular cable television channels like CNN and Cartoon Network, knows how important the human connection is, even in the world of traditional broadcasting.

"Our job is to create fans," said Molly Battin, Executive VP and CMO for Turner. "Fans are much more important than consumers. They share, they debate, they get tattoos. They evangelize, make more fans, and create communities. In a culture that is so polarized, that's a powerful idea. It's time to turn the keys of the marketing kingdom over to the fans."[28]

One of the ways the company does this is by hosting live fan events. Turner Classic Movies has hosted film festivals and a fan cruise for more than a decade. The company more recently started a series of events dedicated to its Adult Swim Channel. The celebration combines the comedy, music, and stars of the channel in quirky activations such as a hot dog ride that bucks like a mechanical bull and a virtual reality experience inspired by "Dream Corp LLC," its show about the goings-on at a sketchy dream-therapy facility.

Every case study I featured in this chapter highlights how live interactions help people connect and belong. Consider how live events and human impressions can build your brand, even if most of your commerce occurs online.

6. Communities defy managerial control.

Brand communities are not corporate assets, so control is an illusion. The whole theme of this book is adjusting to a world where the consumers are in control. Let them lead their communities, too.

Relinquishing control doesn't mean abdicating responsibility. Effective brand stewards participate as community co-creators, nurturing and facilitating communities by creating the conditions in which they can thrive.

Build the space and invite customers to belong ... and lead.

7. Manipulation kills community.

If people sense the purpose of a community is to control them, you'll lose. Remember, this is the end of control!

At some level, people realize you're engaging in an activity to profit from it. But true communities give back to support the leader, not because they're coerced.

"I'm a huge fan of Moog Music," said Keith Jennings, an Atlanta-based marketing executive. "I own their products. I've visited their factory. I drink from a Moog coffee mug. I love how they donate part of their profits to local schools."

"But I don't feel that I belong to Moog. I think Moog belongs to me. I'm a fan of companies that stand for things I believe in. But I'm not interested in entering their marketing narrative. They are entering my narrative."

The funnel has flipped.

8. The mission makes the movement.

Brands that position themselves as essential members of a cultural movement foster emotional connections with consumers. Lululemon is redefining what yoga means with its "This is yoga" campaign. The brand is declaring that yoga today has moved beyond the mat into everyday life. The campaign showcases influencers such as artists, musicians, and entrepreneurs embodying the principles of yoga in their lives.

Essentially, the company is defining a movement that customers can believe in. They're living out their mission, and the mission is the movement.

ARE YOU READY?

Although many brands can benefit from a community strategy, not every company can pull it off. Building a sense of belonging requires an organization-wide commitment and a willingness to work across functional boundaries.

Community is a potent strategy if it's approached with the right mindset and skills. A strong brand community increases customer loyalty, lowers marketing costs, authenticates brand meaning, and yields an influx of ideas to grow the business. When you help people belong, the benefits are irrefutable.

CHAPTER 5

SELF-INTEREST AND THE ARTISANAL BRAND

"The aim of marketing is to make selling superfluous."
—PETER DRUCKER

Once I was on a cross-country flight and settled into my seat for an in-flight movie. I was patronizing Delta Airlines, perhaps the least-crappy of America's selection of crappy airlines, and before the movie, a "pre-roll" story ran promoting Delta's values and vast civic involvement.

With breathless urgency, a female narrator declared: "You're moving at the speed of the world! Look over, look down, and you'll see it. Even when you're sitting back, taking a break, catching your breath, pausing for a moment here in the clouds, you're still going 500 miles an hour. But what does that mean? More than you can dream! Just by getting there, you – yes YOU! – are changing the world!

"Every Delta flight you catch has a butterfly effect. It starts with a click and launches a journey, turns profits into progress, gets into gear, pushes into spaces that connect people, not just destinations. That ticket in your pocket takes a dreamer to college, builds homes, habitats, playgrounds, and pride, honors heroes for their heroism, makes miracles from medicine, supports art that we can see through different eyes.

"We do more than fly planes. We make change. And everything we do is possible because of *you*."

By the measure of most modern marketers (and certainly the advertising agency that produced this video), this exhibits the hallmarks of excellent corporate storytelling and undoubtedly made a lot of executives smile ...

- It's beautifully produced.
- It's emotional.
- It features real people and real stories.
- It connects the company to values and societal good.
- It even takes a stand on social issues, showing moments from a Gay Pride parade and the mention of "dreamers," for example.

But here was my reaction as I watched this lovely video from my freezing-cold seat next to the screaming baby: I. DON'T. CARE.

I just want to escape my exhausted airline reality and see the darn movie, and Delta, you're interrupting me every time you play that stupid video.

I sincerely do not believe you're the Great Charity in the Sky or that this insanely overpriced ticket in my pocket is "taking a dreamer to college." I know deep down you're only saying these things *because you have to*. Somehow this will nudge your stock price and make you feel better about yourself as you check the "social good" box, and I simply do not trust you.

Even if you're truly the Mother Teresa of airlines and demonstrate that you're benevolent and authentic and cool and pride-supporting and home-building, there are enough bad companies out there to make me group you with all the rest of the manipulators, and I'm sorry if I've misjudged you, but that's the way it is. In fact, the only businesses I trust are the ones making a difference and helping people in my local community.

If you really want to change the world, Delta Airlines, do something to really *help me*. Serve me a free, hot meal on this six-hour flight, don't squeeze me into a seat designed for Tyrion Lannister (the small *Game of Thrones* character), and restore some dignity to the process of boarding a plane.

Let's dig below the surface of this example. Am I just a grumpy frequent flyer, or are there clues to bigger consumer trends here? (Spoiler alert: There is a bigger consumer trend here).

Why is the popular notion of corporate "storytelling" so difficult these days? Let's look at the facts.

CORPORATE "MESSAGING" ISN'T BELIEVED

I recently browsed the website of one of the biggest corporate polluters in the world. It's not that the company is inherently evil. They just have a process that requires stripping away virgin forests for their raw materials, turning that into a slush with toxic byproducts, and then spewing tons of chemicals into the air.

But if you look at their website, you would think they were Greenpeace or something. Whales leaping from the ocean! Grazing cows! Splashing waterfalls!

This is a phenomenon known as *greenwashing.* Companies fill their sites with improbable stories of corporate benevolence and stock photos of joyful, racially diverse people leaping in fields of sunflowers, all with the hope of distracting people from reality.

Companies spin the truth. We've been thoroughly conditioned to not believe them, and this is reflected in research like the Edelman Trust Barometer, which shows that trust in businesses has declined precipitously over time and now resides at an all-time low. This implies that no matter how hard you work on the "arc of your story," people probably won't trust it. I mean, whales? C'mon.

It's one of the weirdest trends: Companies are spending more on cause marketing, charitable giving is on the rise, social media has forced more transparency, and yet trust in companies is *going down.*

Compare this Delta video example with the North Face "Question Madness" content I covered in Chapter 4. The North Face made their customers the stars and invited them to belong. Delta Airlines is still operating under the delusion that they're in control by claiming *they're* the hero of the story. That video is essentially saying, "Look how great we are!"

I had a little fun picking on Delta Airlines (love you, Delta!), but the problem is nearly universal. We don't believe *anybody* preaching from an ivory tower (even Ivory!). And the truth is, you're not special. Your customers probably don't believe you or your stock photos, either.

CORPORATE STORYTELLING ISN'T NATIVE

Another reason corporate storytelling may not work anymore is because these tales rarely fit into the flow of a person's native content stream.

Do this simple test. Quickly scroll through your Instagram feed without concentrating on who posted the photo and try to guess which posts are sponsored content and which ones are from your friends. I can do it almost every time without fail. Why? Because the sponsored pictures stick out like a long-tailed cat in a room full of rocking chairs – they still look like ads, not photos from your friends.

Most corporate content still looks like corporate content. As soon as my Spidey-senses detect even the lightest touch of PR spin, a too-perfect photo of employees in matching outfits or writing that has been drained of life by the legal-approval strainer, the story is no longer a story. It's an ad. A company may call it a story, but the world sees it as an ad.

And we generally don't like ads. We avoid them, block them, skip them, and walk out of the room to get a drink when they appear. Most corporate storytelling is still an ad because it is not native to a person's normal content experience.

IF IT'S NOT LOCAL, IT'S OVER

Carla Buzasi, managing director for trend-spotting company WGSN, recently reported on the idea that power in the world is shifting to "localvists."

A localvist is somebody leading real activism at a local level.

We've been in a prolonged period of *slacktivism* where working for change meant "liking" the Facebook page of a social cause. But the localvists are fed up with the toxic, polarized world and have learned that they can work for real change.

Columnist and NPR commentator David Brooks wrote:[29] "Localism is thriving because many cities have more coherent identities than the nation as a whole. It is thriving because while national politics takes place through the filter of the media circus, local politics by and large does not. It is thriving because we're in an era of low social trust. People really have faith only in the relationships right around them, the change agents who are on the ground."

This is not an age-related trend. It's happening everywhere because there's a feeling that there is a real possibility to create change in our world. This movement isn't just aimed at governments, either. It's also affecting banking, corporations, nonprofit institutions, and anybody else standing in the way of progress, inclusiveness, and personal freedom.

Localism is a signature characteristic of the Third Rebellion and one of the most significant trends impacting our businesses today. It literally flips the power structure. For decades, money, talent, and power have flowed from the corporate centers. But under localism, the power center is at the tip of a shovel, where the actual work is being done, and with those who know how stuff gets accomplished in a specific place. Success isn't measured by the size of your advertising budget but rather by how sincerely you can connect.

Advertising is impersonal, uniform, and intrusive. The localist requires connection that is relational, affectionate, and based on reciprocity and trust.

Localists don't believe corporate stories because they don't believe anything they can't see happening in their community. They have to witness action that supports their self-interests, not just hear plastic words from some faraway advertising agency. Research shows 58 percent of adults don't trust a brand until they've seen "real world proof" that it has kept its promises.[30]

ARTISANAL MARKETING

Marketing must become *artisanal.* If you represent a brand that people tangibly believe in, they are willing to fight for you and even pay more for your product.

"Artisanal" is one of those words that has been beat to a pulp on the web, like "personal branding" and "best-selling." And yet there aren't many worthy synonyms for this essential idea. Successful marketing in the future will have to be presented in a way that is unquestionably authentic, local, personalized, and even handcrafted. It will have to make a difference that people can see and experience.

Artisanal marketing has these qualities:

- It is so compellingly authentic, believable, and natural that people will want to carry your story forward. Your customers don't want to be bought, and they'll have a negative reaction to anyone they suspect is trying to sell them something. Your story has to be true – and not just cleared-by-the-lawyers true. It has to respect your audience's intelligence.

- It provides an experience that is unique, remarkable, and meaningful on a personal level.

- It dispenses an obvious benefit that connects to a person's self-interest. It tangibly helps a person or their community make money, save money, protect the environment, become healthier, become happier, be more entertained, feel more self-esteem, and so on.

How does a global mega-brand like Delta Airlines adopt an artisanal marketing strategy? Not without an overhaul of its entire business culture, I'm afraid.

Companies and brands that seek quick and impersonal transactions with us tempt us to leave them every day. By contrast, the rules in a communal relationship rely on responsiveness to each other's needs. We take care of each other. We are in it together. We belong. We don't keep pressing for the quick sale.

Not many businesses can afford to operate on strictly a "communal" basis, nor do they need to. As I said in a previous chapter, sometimes you don't want "community." You just want a hamburger. But we are starting to see even large companies figure out the artisanal marketing model.

Let's look at a few examples.

"Artisanal is in our DNA"

I was waiting for my turn to speak at a marketing conference in Minneapolis (such a beautiful city!) when an organizer sitting next to me asked if I knew about a local furniture business called Room & Board. I did not.

With unrelenting excitement (about furniture?), he told me how this company had partnered with many of the small family businesses that had been decimated in the 1980s and 1990s when American furniture manufacturing moved offshore. Room & Board is helping these artisans create modern new designs based on traditional American styles and then market their products through an eCommerce site and nationwide network of stores.

I didn't live in Minneapolis and wasn't in the market for furniture, but I was intrigued. What made this company so special that this business executive was enthusiastically telling me their story? I visited their website and was entranced by the inspiring tales – told through blog posts and videos – of how this company was single-handedly resurrecting the American furniture industry.

I wanted to know more, so I interviewed Gene Wilson, the company's director of merchandising. I discovered that Room & Board is a big company with a human-centered and local view of the world.

"We were one of the original disruptors," Gene said. "Our founder John Gabbert had built a successful career in the furniture business but had had enough with the constant sales pressure and never-ending promotions. So he left a successful family business to start his own furniture company that was built on a new dynamic.

"Instead of sourcing everything from China or another foreign country, he reached out to the talented artisanal furniture craftsmen that were struggling when the industry moved overseas.

"He partnered with them to revive the American furniture industry. He worked with them on new designs and business plans, sometimes on the back of a napkin. We put our salespeople on a salary so the emphasis was on serving customers, not selling something. We don't have seasonal promotions like other companies and our prices are guaranteed for a year, so our customers can buy furniture on their own timeline. Our designs are craft-based following the American Amish and Shaker traditions. We use natural materials and stress simplicity and functionality."

When I visited their Atlanta store, the salesperson, Elizabeth Caruso, explained that the company refurbishes historic buildings in aging city centers. The structure I was standing in had been a large meatpacking plant, and she showed me the remnants of meat smokers poking through a showroom of couches.

Instead of sitting empty after store hours, she explained that the company offers workshops, talks, and community events, lending their beautiful space to build local goodwill.

Elizabeth, who has worked at the Atlanta retail location for nine years, was able to tell me the detailed stories behind every piece of furniture – the family businesses and their history, the glass blowers, the story behind the wood selections, and the small American steel makers who contributed to the rugged furniture on display.

I was particularly taken with a handmade cabinet that had an extraordinary rough-hewn look. Elizabeth explained that the cabinet had been made through a partnership with the U.S. Forest Service and the city of Baltimore. A local artisan had hired people with barriers to employment to reclaim material that would have been taken to a landfill. The beautiful aged pine for the cabinet I admired had been salvaged from roof decking of row houses along the Baltimore waterfront. Some of the wood panels dated back to the 1800s. It wasn't just a cabinet. It was history.

Today, nearly 50 artisan partners throughout the country fulfill orders across America for Room & Board.

The company has almost no formal marketing or advertising because the great story of their community connections keeps spreading, fueling rapid growth. "We believe in transparency and keeping our customers, our partners, and employees happy," Gene told me. "Word-of-mouth referrals are big for us. People see the impact we're having on their communities and they keep spreading the word. Artisanal is in our DNA."

Room & Board is a big company offering tangible value on a local level. It's value people can see, touch, and take pride in.

Scaling personal experiences

There's probably no more mundane product than a bank-issued credit card, but Mastercard CMO Raja Rajamannar is helping an established brand rise above the noise of endless credit card advertising by creating artisanal experiences aimed squarely at consumer self-interests.

"Storytelling is dead, at least in the commercial context," he said in an interview.[31] "Consumers look at advertising as an annoyance, as an interruption to their experience. They irritate them. So the initial solution is the DVR where consumers can jump over ads. Now we have ad blockers. If you look at the scale of ad blocking ... it's huge!

"Beyond that, people are willing to pay for an ad-free experience. People are screaming in your face saying 'I don't want your stupid ads, and we say, oh no, we'll just show you better ads. It's a foolish response on our part. Consumers have learned to tune us out. Today, the focus can't be on storytelling, it's on story*making*."

"We're creating experiences for consumers at scale. For example, for our wealthier customers, we have experiences called Priceless Cities, which are truly once-in-a-lifetime events. Experiences like visiting a World Heritage Site by yourself without the crowds, exclusive concert tickets, or watching a sunset from the top of a pyramid. We have 750 different experiences now, and they are constantly changing because we want to create excitement for our customers on a continuous basis.

"And after you experience one of these events, your whole neighborhood is going to know about it because you're going to talk about this life experience. Our best customers also become our brand ambassadors. Now our customers are the storytellers, not ads. It's word-of-mouth marketing on steroids."

Artisanal tech[32]

Even the savviest observer of the Japanese video game giant Nintendo couldn't have predicted that its most popular interactive gaming experience would not involve a virtual reality headset or a new Mario game but rather perforated cardboard, colorful string, elastic bands, and plastic grommets.

These resolutely low-tech items are the stuff of Labo (short for "laboratory"), a series of add-ons for Nintendo's popular Switch handheld console.

As much homemade craft projects as they are games, Labo's do-it-yourself kits let you fold cardboard parts into smart toys that you can engage with using the Switch. The $70 Variety Kit provides the makings of a piano and a fishing rod, along with a house, a motorbike, and two radio-controlled cars. Labo's $80 Robot Kit contains parts for a visor and backpack that, once built, turn the wearer into a Transformers-style automaton.

There's even a simple programming feature that allows users to devise new functionalities, like using the Robot Kit backpack to steer a car (I'll pass, thank you).

With these kits, Nintendo is building emotional connection beyond their game characters. They're giving their fans a way to touch their product, build something like a craftsman, and proudly talk about it with their friends.

I think this is a cool idea, and I want to give you something to play with, too. Visit *businessesGROW.com/rebellion* to download an awesome Marketing Rebellion coloring book hand-drawn for you by my friend, Paris Woodhull.

Make me a hero

One of my all-time favorite marketing case studies comes from Nike. For the last few FIFA World Cups, Nike was not an official sponsor but stole all the buzz through epic marketing ideas that created enormous online conversations ... at a fraction of the cost of sponsorship.

Through the miracle of social media, I had a chance to meet the brilliant man behind the on-the-ground activation at the 2014 World Cup in Brazil, Fabio Tambosi (who is now with Adidas in Germany).

Fabio spent some time with me at my home and gave me this behind-the-scenes story of his success:

"The only way to become a meaningful brand and rise above all this noise in the world is to know and understand the consumers' deepest self-interests and then anchor the marketing strategy in this knowledge. When the team was developing a strategy for the World Cup, an important insight that rose from our research was personified by a 17-year old fellow named Bruno who said, *'Don't give me more heroes, make me one.'*

"We realized that consumers were ready to be challenged and were inviting the brand into their lives. They were asking for a platform to become better soccer players, instead of just seeing their soccer heroes glorified on TV. This insight fueled how we took our messages to the streets and built an entirely new consumer-centric journey.

"The quintessential questions we asked ourselves were, 'How are we helping them feel like heroes?' and 'Are we treating our consumers as well as we treat the pro athletes?'

"The big YouTube videos dropped by the brand – mini-movies, really – were the most obvious manifestations of our consumer insight. These were highly produced pieces featuring appearances by many soccer stars. It took a lot to make them, but it cost a fraction of what a World Cup sponsorship or ad campaign would have entailed.

"In a video called *Winner Stays,* a 17-year-old *futebol-aficionado* became the hero who stepped up when everything was on the line and the stakes were the highest. Why? Because that is what the greatest do. That's the feeling we wanted to capture.

"Our campaign to make people feel heroic went down into the very heart of our key cities, neighborhoods, and streets where our customers lived, even the favelas of Rio de Janeiro. We held clinics, we sponsored tournaments, we had workshops for coaches. We customized locker room and game time experiences like what the pros would have. We even handed out our latest gear in the neighborhoods and let them feel what it's like to be a soccer star seeing new equipment for the first time.

"Today, marketers can't just be in a city. You have to be *of the city.*"

Powerful words. The lesson is that you have to create meaningful experiences that appeal to your customers' foundational self-interests, in this case being seen in a heroic way. Your customers have to experience you where they live, believe you where they live, and trust you where they live.

The worship of scale

At this point I'm imagining that some of you are getting upset about this whole idea of abandoning the comparatively easy world of "advertising impressions" for the much more difficult one of local, artisanal "human impressions." I warned you ... the days of the marketing easy button are over.

But before you march on my office with torches and pitchforks, consider your options. Are you going to keep doing what you've always done and melt away like the Wicked Witch of the West, or will you vanquish your competitors by re-tuning and embracing the chaos of these undeniable realities?

Of course, there will always be room for brand storytelling in some manner. It's important. But I don't think it can be overemphasized that we're in a period of remarkable change when it comes to consumer views of brands, marketing, and trust. In the heart of the fake news era, we need to rethink how we tell our story, where we tell it, what we tell ... and most important, *who* tells it.

One of the challenges of the artisanal marketing approach is that it can't be scaled as easily as an ad. In fact, scale is the *opposite* of artisanal, and unfortunately, most marketing departments are built to worship scale.

"Marketers tend to think in terms of buckets," said Jeremy Floyd, who has been a CMO for a number of startups. "What happened in that demographic bucket, or that persona bucket, or that regional bucket? But the audience isn't a bucket, it's a person. When we treat people like they're in a bucket, then they're no longer human to us. Marketers want to scale their workflow at every level. Customers want the opposite of that."

The Knoxville soap company found success where Ivory never could by showing up at community meetings to tell their story.

It takes extraordinary effort for Room & Board to make handcrafted American furniture instead of shipping a design off to China for mass production.

Mastercard is going the extra mile to make personal dreams come true instead of asking people "What's in your wallet?" (over and over and over).

Nintendo is a high-tech company focusing on the basic human emotions that come from holding something you've crafted yourself.

Fabio Tambosi worked for a massive company, Nike, but his success came from taking their World Cup message to the neighborhoods of Brazil where the brand became "of the city."

Companies are tuning in to this "constant human need" of local self-interests. Look carefully and you'll see artisanal marketing happening all around you.

- Examine the tags sewn into T-shirts made by Known Supply and you'll find something unexpected – a woman's signature. Names like Lamunu Kevin, Paolo Perales, and Thangamani, a seamstress from South India. Type her name into the company's website to see her picture and read her story. "My theory was that if we could understand the people behind our product, we would think about purchasing products differently," founder Kohl Crecelius said. "We would realize that our story is bound up in the story of others."[33]

- New retailers are using technology and eCommerce to provide custom experiences like your own fragrance (from Olfactory) or handmade shoes (from Awl & Sundry). A new brick-and-mortar store, Consortium, specializes in these artisanal, made-to-order fashion brands. Both Nike and Adidas have opened flagship stores that allow customers to design and manufacture their own sneakers in an hour.

- As local-sourcing claims are increasingly in doubt and the "farm-to-table" descriptor has become overused, chefs are now establishing their own farms or forming long-term partnerships with existing ones to make good on a promise of using local ingredients in their dishes.

- American Eagle, a leading casual wear retailer for teens, has set up a "maker's shop" within stores where customers can modify their jeans with patches and other alterations.

- Pepsi acquired a small company that allows customers to make their own fizzy sodas at home.

- DBS Bank in Singapore recently decided to expand to India, where it didn't have any customer base. Instead of spending on advertising throughout the country, it partnered with a popular coffeehouse to create a branchless bank, where customers can enroll and start banking immediately on their mobile devices. The friendly, local coffee-chain partnership has proved to be far more effective than traditional branch offices. The approach established them as a trusted, caring part of the community, and within a year, DBS had 1.2 million new banking customers in the country.[34]

And yes, there's even a U.S. airline having success with an artisanal marketing approach. "We're a large company but we have a local attitude by tapping into local language and customs," said Heather Berko, who leads marketing efforts at JetBlue. "We spend a lot of time talking about what it means to be in one of our destination cities so we can develop deep roots in those communities.

"One example is being sensitive to a stressful time for our friends in Boston – Move-In Day. Since Boston is such a college town, more than 80 percent of all apartment leases in the city change on September 1 every year. Everybody seems to be moving! We decided to offer a special promotion so customers could have a chance to get out of town and avoid the congestion. We want to show that we're a neighbor, we're part of Boston, and we understand the city.

"Another example of how we literally get into our customer neighborhoods was building a pop-up "Jet Boo" house in neighborhoods to hand out candy during Halloween.

Everybody knows the best houses give out full-size candy and we did that, becoming the most popular house on the street! This also helped get our local crewmembers into the community to have face-to-face conversations with our customers outside the hustle and bustle of the airport."

Don't be in a city. Be of the city.

Give up control. Make the customer the hero.

Get down to the neighborhoods, the favelas, the community meetings. Go right to the tip of the shovel.

Find your customer's deepest self-interests and then connect at the street level to show that you understand and care.

CHAPTER 6

VALUES-BASED MARKETING AND THE SEARCH FOR MEANING

*"Companies attempting to 'position' themselves
need to take a position."*

—THE CLUETRAIN MANIFESTO

In Chapter 1, I reference the seminal marketing textbook, *Principles of Marketing,* written by Dr. Philip Kotler. For my research on *Marketing Rebellion,* I went to eBay and discovered a copy of the original edition from my college days. As I sentimentally thumbed through the book, I was struck by how much of the classic text is still relevant, even in this disruptive age. But there was something obviously missing – a marketing truth Dr. Kotler didn't see coming.

One of the most famous marketing mantras is the importance of the "Four Ps." To assess a market and create demand, you must consider the combination of Product, Promotion, Price, and Place (or Placement).

But in the Third Rebellion, there's another P that must be considered in the classic toolkit: Purpose.

We live in the most prosperous age in history. Many of us have the basics covered – food on the table, education, housing, and economic security. We even have Oprah and Netflix. The next thing we want to achieve is significance. What is our purpose? Are we making a difference? Do our actions matter and echo into the distance? Can we connect our choices to positive impact in our world?

Author Bernadette Jiwa proposes that we live in an era when meaning is more important than money. "The Meaning Economy has created a new customer who is drawn to brands that enable them to express their values," she said. "We know that how we spend our money and which causes we champion are votes for the future we want to see. We support businesses that are generous and mindful of the impact they make. We're moving towards the formulation of a new value equation – one that rewards work that is carried out with heart and rewards businesses that are driven by purpose before profits."[35]

Since 2005, the importance of "meaning" in driving job selection has grown steadily.[36] Today, 9 out of 10 Americans would take a lower-paying job if it meant they could do meaningful work that contributes to society. Meaning is the new money. Meaning is the new marketing.

I've written about how control of the customer journey has moved from companies to consumers. This created the shop-around culture and an evaporation of loyalty to brands most of the time. In this chapter, I discuss why meaning-centered marketing is the one strategy that still earns loyalty.

Let's start by dissecting the business strategy for a common fashion item – denim jeans – and discover how retailer American Eagle is rewriting the marketing playbook.

PURPOSE AND POLITICS

Futurist Faith Popcorn said, "Advertising is dead. Over. Culture is the new media. Don't buy an ad. Put your brand's belief into the culture."[37]

American Eagle is certainly a brand that subscribes to that new marketing vision.

AE, a Pittsburgh-based company, is the second-largest jean seller in America.[38] Founded in 1977 as a niche clothing boutique, the chain is now commonly found in U.S. shopping malls, with nearly 1,000 stores. While it sells a variety of clothing items, its primary focus is providing everything denim for high school- and college-aged Americans, which is a lot.

Because of its strong relationship with the youth market, we can view AE as a bellwether company when it comes to the consumer changes simmering on the edge of the Third Rebellion.

The company spends an extraordinary amount of money on research and has even hired teens for their executive office to keep the company from doing anything that might alienate its core audience. To see what the next generation expects from marketers, let's take a look at some of the initiatives AE has launched in the past couple of years:

- After a shocking and much-publicized shooting at a Florida high school, the company sent an email blast to its customers encouraging them to participate in anti-gun rallies. It posted a photo of a large rally to its 2.7 million Instagram followers.

- AE stopped using photo-shopped images of models with unachievable body types. It launched a platform called AE X Me, which taps real customers, based on their Instagram posts, to become brand ambassadors. The photos in the campaign are shot in the schools and gritty neighborhoods of real customers.

- The brand launched a special project called "It Gets Better" to place a spotlight on civil liberties and empowering LGBTQ youth. It created a special fashion line called "The Pride Collection" to fund efforts supporting civil liberties. The company is using transsexual and same-sex couples in its ads, proclaiming, "Love is love."

This is not your typical marketing to sell denim jeans, is it?

Predictably, these initiatives have been controversial. On Instagram, it was clear the brand had alienated quite a few people. "Stay out of politics, and do what you're good at ... selling clothes," one person commented on the brand's anti-gun post. In fact, there have been live protests against the brand in some cities.

Why would a brand invite this controversy?

Because this is what its customers demand.

The company's decision to support the progressive values of its audience did not come casually. American Eagle researchers found that young adults think of themselves as politically involved, connected, and diverse. That diversity extends to ethnicity, sexuality, and even body image.

"We try and speak to the politics of this generation," said global brand president Chad Kessler in an interview. "Gen Z is the most diverse generation in American history. They have this expectation that brands will reflect this diversity."

In 2018, the marketing world witnessed an explosive example of brand-political alignment when Nike introduced an advertising campaign and new clothing line featuring Colin Kaepernick, an NFL quarterback who kneeled as a sign of protest when the American National Anthem played before games. This act polarized both fans and the owners of professional football league teams. Was he a courageous civil rights activist or disrespecting the country's flag, heritage, and veterans?

When the marketing campaign was announced, outraged citizen groups posted videos of people burning piles of Nike shoes and athletic wear.

In business school, most of us grew up on lessons from the famous economist Milton Friedman and his admonition that a firm should only engage in activities that increase shareholder value. We learned that business was one thing, and society was another. He said, "There is one and only one social responsibility of business – to use its resources and engage in activities designed to increase its profits so long as it stays within the rules of the game..."

Obviously, the rules of the game have changed.

Of course, businesses still have to make a profit. Companies are an accumulation of human beings who want to survive and thrive. In fact, in a public company, there is a *mandate* to survive. Survival, in corporate terms, means profits, but today it also means being ethical, treating people well, and taking responsibility for the planet you're inhabiting. I suppose we should be grateful for the Third Rebellion, which is demanding a new, more enlightened path toward those profits.

Companies are aligning their commercial activities with larger social and cultural values because they know that it's good for business in the long run.

MEANING MATTERS

These examples of creating marketing campaigns based on meaning are more than short-term gimmicks or publicity stunts. Taking a stand and connecting to a consumer's values may be the last great loyalty strategy we have left.

According to research published in the *Harvard Business Review*, there are three common myths around customer loyalty:[39]

1. **Myth:** Customers want to have relationships with brands. **Truth:** 77 percent don't want a relationship. What they really want are discounts.

2. **Myth:** Customer engagement builds relationships. **Truth:** No, it doesn't. Your customers already suffer from information overload.

3. **Myth:** The more interactions the better. **Truth:** Wrong. There's no correlation between the number of interactions with a customer and loyalty.

The research showed only one consideration is far and away the primary driver of customer loyalty: shared meaning.

A shared meaning is a belief that both the brand and consumer have about a brand's values or broad philosophy. We see this insight translated in the American Eagle and Nike strategies, and many other companies are baking strong value-based brand stands into their messaging:

- H&M's "Conscious Collection" of eco-friendly clothing features 100-percent reclaimed nylon fiber from fishnets and other nylon waste. H&M was one of the first fashion retailers to make its supply chain transparent, and it constantly monitors the working conditions of the factories where its products are produced.

- Airbnb aired an ad during the Super Bowl to protest U.S. immigration policies. The ad, called "We Accept," showed a montage of people of different nationalities along with the words: "We believe no matter who you are, where you're from, who you love, or who you worship, we all belong. The world is more beautiful the more you accept."

- P&G launched "We See Equal," a campaign designed to fight gender bias and workplace inequality.

These brands are stepping out and becoming more socially progressive because their customers are.

Research conducted by Edelman[40] showed that 67 percent of consumers will try a brand for the first time solely because they agree with its position on a controversial topic, and 65 percent said they will *not* buy a brand when it stays silent on an issue they consider important.

The study, which polled 8,000 people in eight countries, found that a company's position on a social issue can drive purchase intent just as much as the features of a product.

"People want to be associated with brands that stand for something or are a force for change," said Richard Edelman, the firm's chief executive.

When brands speak out, they are rewarded. Nearly a quarter of all consumers will pay at least a 25 percent premium when their values align with a brand, and 51 percent will buy the brand exclusively based on shared values.

The numbers are convincing. Taking a stand – with due diligence – is one of the few remaining paths to consumer loyalty, advocacy, and even premium pricing.

YOUR COMPANY MAY DEPEND ON IT

It's not just customers who are demanding social and political activism. Pressure is coming from the financial markets as well.[41]

In 2018, investment firm BlackRock shook Wall Street with an edict to business leaders that companies need to do more than make profits – they also need to contribute to society if they want to receive support from the investment company.

BlackRock has the clout to make this demand. The firm manages more than $6 trillion in investments, making it the largest investor in the world, and it has an oversized influence on whether directors are voted on and off boards.

The BlackRock CEO wrote, "Society is demanding that companies, both public and private, serve a social purpose. To prosper over time, every company must not only deliver financial performance, but also show how it makes a positive contribution to society."

He said that if a company doesn't engage with the community and have a sense of purpose, "it will ultimately lose the license to operate from key stakeholders."

The New York Times called this a watershed moment, one that raises all sorts of questions about the very nature of capitalism. The world's largest investor saying that companies have to be about more than money – and declaring that it plans to hold them accountable – is a bracing example of the evolution of corporate America and the undeniable impact of the Third Rebellion.

"We are even seeing the values discussion coming up in procurement quotes from our customers," said Allison Herzog, director of global digital strategy for Dell Technologies. "Today, customers want to be aligned with companies that have a demonstrated purpose, and that has to be aligned up and down the company."[42]

CONNECTING THE DOTS

In Chapter 3, I make a case for the importance of *human impressions* in the long-term marketing strategy of a company. People don't trust companies. People trust people. That trust must be integrated into how we connect with customers going forward.

When companies speak out, consumers want it to come from the top, from the human beings running the company.

The majority of consumers – 93 percent – said they're more likely to purchase when a chief executive issues statements about pressing societal issues and they agree with that sentiment.[43]

That human connection, that human voice, provides the gravitas and compassion behind the statement. Today, being a leader is more than overseeing a growing enterprise and a strong balance sheet. It means you *are* the brand.

BUT DO MARKETERS CARE?

We've seen that most companies have been slow to connect to the new consumer realities.

Here's yet another sign that the marketing profession is falling behind: Researchers from Duke University and Deloitte[44] found that 83 percent of chief marketing officers don't think it's appropriate for a brand to take a controversial stand, and if you remove one outlier group (universities), the number is 90 percent.

Here we go again.

Consumers say: "Take a stand. We'll be loyal."

The financial markets say: "Take a stand, or we won't back you."

Marketers say: "No thanks."

Who do you think will win in the end? If you answered "consumers," then you're learning your lessons well my friend!

I'm not necessarily poking fun at these marketing leaders. I can empathize with them. I'm sure there isn't one CMO in the world who has this objective in their job description: "Anger your customer base so much they burn your products in the streets."

And when you take a political stand, that is certainly a risk:

- When Delta Airlines took a stand against the National Rifle Association, many frequent flyers were up in arms. (Ummm ... perhaps that's a poor choice of words, but you know what I mean.)

- McDonald's created a special logo to celebrate International Women's Day, which sparked protests over the company's low pay policies.

- #BoycottKeurig became a top trending topic on social media after the home brewing company crumbled under political pressure and removed ads from a popular conservative talk show. Individuals began posting videos in which they destroyed their Keurig machines in a visually impactful brand boycott.

THE ISSUE OF RELEVANCE

Despite the risk, taking a stand may be a vital opportunity to refresh an aging brand and find new relevance with consumers.

The Enso Agency scored 150 brands according to how consumers identify their purpose, the extent to which that purpose aligns with the consumers' own values, and the degree to which it motivates advocacy and purchases.[45]

The results show striking differences between generations. For example, Proctor & Gamble is ranked number 12 on the list of respected companies by baby boomers (over 55 years of age), but it has a lowly ranking of 103 with millennials (18-34 years old) – a huge disparity, even though the company spends more than $7 billion each year in advertising

Many P&G brands like Ivory have been struggling, and the company risks continued declining sales and eroding brand equity unless it can appeal to younger consumers. Similarly, AAA, Chevrolet, Pfizer, and Samsung are brands that have significantly lower rankings by millennials than by baby boomers.

There are a few reasons why brands may underperform with younger people. In some cases, products become more relevant at older ages – Pfizer's pharmaceutical products, for example. In other cases, cultural mega-trends are against brands, like the declining importance of car ownership to younger people (affecting AAA and Chevrolet).

But most brands do not have these forces working against them. They may be underperforming because the brand is becoming irrelevant. 68 percent of millennials say, "Creating change in the world is a personal goal that I actively pursue," but that value is expressed by just 42 percent of baby boomers.

Meaning matters to the millennials. How can age-challenged brands become relevant to younger people? In short, by developing more meaning.

When we look at the brands performing well, many of them have a clear, values-based mission. The Honest Company's stand for product transparency and healthy families has helped it to a 34 ranking for millennials, while it's number 84 for boomers. Starbucks has taken strong stands for ethical sourcing, social justice, and environmental progress. That brand stand helped it achieve a ranking of 25 with millennials versus 111 for boomers.

And yes, even P&G is catching on. The Always line of feminine products stepped out with a campaign called "Like A Girl," turning a phrase that had become an insult into an empowering message. The long-established brand now ranks 29 with millennials.

In a classic *Harvard Business Review* article, Theodore Levitt asked the famous question, "What business are you in?" His point was that the railroads thought they were in the railroad business, but they were upended by cars, trucks, and the new highway system. Had they seen that they were actually in the transportation business and not just the railroad business, they could have seized the opportunities that automobiles presented. He called this inability of companies to see beyond their vertical "marketing myopia."[46]

For the brands that are aging their way out of relevance, history is repeating itself. Some companies are no longer in the product or service business. They're in the purpose business. The marketing myopia persists. CMOs may not be driving the needed changes because they think they're merely selling a tangible product.

IS THIS STRATEGY RIGHT FOR EVERY BUSINESS?

The evidence is in.

Consumers of the Third Rebellion want us to take a stand and fortify the meaning in their lives through the communion of shared values. Does this mean every company has to create meaning through controversial stands?

No. Of course not.

Sometimes we just want a car wash because our automobile is filthy or a hamburger because it tastes so good. Hold the onions and angst please!

This book is a road map, not a manifesto. You have to choose what's right for you, and most important, what's right for your customer base.

All I ask is that you wake up to the realities of our world and see them as opportunities instead of threats. Make a logical decision that's best for your organization with eyes wide open.

While it's true that values-based marketing might mean taking a stand that can anger some people, aligning with values and providing meaning doesn't necessarily have to be divisive.

My favorite meaning-based marketing case study is Heineken's "Worlds Apart" social-experiment-turned-video-commercial. I encourage you to watch it on YouTube.

In the experiment, two strangers are paired up to build a table together, and the activity helps them have a little fun and get to know each other. After a level of respect and rapport is reached, it's revealed to the strangers that they hold drastically opposing views on divisive, hot-button topics such as transgender rights, climate change, and feminism.

The participants are then given the choice to either stay and talk it over with a Heineken beer in hand, or part ways. After some excruciating tension, everyone decides to stay, and the audience is gifted with hopeful scenes demonstrating humanity's capacity for kindness, empathy, and acceptance – despite our differences.

This is great storytelling that shows how the world can come together when we think it's falling apart. And that kind of meaning is accessible to any business.

You don't have to take out ads about gun control or hire an outspoken celebrity to show you care. Every company has an opportunity to offer customers hope, love, and unity like Heineken did.

YOUR VALUES-BASED MARKETING STRATEGY

If a values-based marketing strategy seems right for you, I've examined dozens of success stories (and failures) and believe there are some common themes that can help you give it your best shot.

What steps should you consider if it makes sense for your brand to take a stand?

1. Be clear on your values.

David Armano, Global Strategy Director of Edelman, said there are three things a company needs to do to get clear on its own internal value system:

1. **Discover your purpose.** Why do you do what you do? Start there. Is this grounded in tradition alone, or does the company's reason for being need to be updated with a modern lens?

2. **Validate social tension.** Once you're clear on your values, how does this connect to your customers? What's getting in the way of the customers living out

their values? Taking aim at this societal tension and aligning it with the brand's passion leads to a sense of purpose and direction for activation.

3. **Use your unique voice.** Having a "true north" expressed as purpose can become a differentiator if the intent is right and the expression fits the brand's mission and personality. Ultimately, the potential of purpose is to act as a filter for all actions and communications from the brand.

2. Create rock-solid alignment.

Marketing today is not just about your "why," it's also about your customer's "why."

Of course it makes sense for Patagonia to take a stand against legislation that opens up protected land to development. Of course it makes sense for Airbnb to connect on issues of public housing. Of course American Eagle is going to take a position that empowers the treasured values of its teen customers.

When these companies take a stand, it's logical because the position aligns with their core mission and the values of their customers.

Brand identity has been the single most important factor for increasing sales and ensuring growth since the dawn of capitalism. But a brand today is no longer just a symbol, logo, or tagline. A brand must include the promise of what the customer will experience emotionally and even politically.

3. Take a measured risk.

If you decide to take a stand, you can't change your mind or you risk becoming a meme – or worse. This decision must be carefully considered based on research and insight.

You'd better believe Nike ran the numbers before making their bold political move with Colin Kaepernick.

Two-thirds of Nike customers are under the age of 35. A large-scale study of the political views of this demographic showed that nearly 80 percent hold liberal to moderate views on social issues. A young consumer who can afford $200 shoes likely has substantial disposable income and lives in a city. The term for this demographic? Progressive.

Nike knew there would be a backlash and risked a sizable portion of its business to strengthen the relationship with the young consumers who account for 90 percent of its revenue.

And, indeed, there was a backlash. In one day, Nike's market value dropped by nearly $4 billion dollars. But one week later, its market value was even higher than before the volatile campaign began.

The math? Nike just did it.

4. Be congruent.

Political positioning tends to backfire if it appears that the stance is a one-off or an attempt by the company to selfishly grab attention. In every case the brand stand strategy has succeeded, the company has demonstrated its values in many ways, continuously over time.

A values-based marketing strategy will only work if the values are aligned not just with the consumers but also with the *actions* of the company itself.

Human rights, racism, civil liberties, global warming – these are extremely complex issues that aren't going to be solved through a sensational ad campaign.

American Eagle demonstrated leadership by placing its money, its influence, and its workforce in service of the values it also displays in its marketing.

Marketing isn't just about *making* promises, it's about *keeping* promises.

5. Emphasize action over words.

Most people believe that brands have more power to solve social issues than the government.

But they want more than words in an ad campaign. Companies need to be active and visible in their customer communities, fighting for their preferred causes.

Microsoft Chairman Satya Nadella wrote: "Multinationals can no longer be the memes they've become – soulless, bloodless entities that enter a nation or a region simply to take rent from the locals. The job of a multinational is more important than ever. It needs to operate everywhere in the world, contributing to local communities in positive ways – sparking growth, competitiveness, and opportunity for all. How can we help our local partners and startups grow? How can we help the public sector become more efficient? How can we help solve the most pressing issues in society?"[47]

6. Take care with creative treatments.

The presentation of these brand/consumer values must be confident but sensitive. It would be arrogant for a brand to suggest they are a solution. They can be a bridge to a solution or a platform for discussion. This must be supported through expert creative treatments.

Nothing can undo a brand image faster than good intentions presented in an inappropriate perspective.

7. Be ready for the heat.

The organization must be completely aligned at every level and prepared for repercussions when, predictably, certain consumer groups rebel against the idea. Can your corporate culture withstand a controversy? Can your career?

And don't forget to be prepared for the *internal* reaction. If you take a stand that your customers love but your employees hate, can you still operate as a company?

Employee voices are increasingly playing a role in whether companies take sides on political issues. Tech companies, for example, had little to gain strategically by opposing U.S. immigration policies. But Microsoft and Google found it impossible to remain silent in the face of employee demands for a response to what they regarded as an assault on company values.

8. Consider the first-move advantage.

If your customers expect you to take a position to align with their values and you don't, that is, in effect, taking a stand.

It may also make you vulnerable. What's the risk of not taking a stand on an issue and then having your competitor roll out a meaning-based campaign?

Nike made a bold move. Would a values-based marketing campaign by a competitor like Adidas or Under Armour seem unoriginal, or even desperate?

There are only so many "values" to go around. American Eagle's research led them to a highly focused strategy supporting gun control and civil liberties. I don't think a competing retailer in their category could now mimic their aggressive and consistent strategy. AE is owning the hearts of core customers by aligning with their values and by *being the first to do it*.

I want to emphasize once again that I'm not being prescriptive. You have to make the right decisions for your business. I'm just laying out the options.

9. Have a crisis plan.

In our fast-changing and complex world, it's impossible to prepare for every eventuality. It's difficult for even seasoned professionals to predict what could suddenly ignite into controversy. So, hope for the best and plan for the worst. If your company decides to take a controversial stand, have an executive team and PR professionals standing by for a few days after the announcement.

GET INVOLVED

Taking a stand that demonstrates your values doesn't have to be expensive, risky, or complicated.

Find groups in your community that share your values and need your help. Sponsor their events, donate your services, and better yet, show up. Let people see how you care. Don't just lend a hand. *Be the hand.* That's what people want and need from you.

The most human company wins.

Go. Be that company for your community.

CHAPTER 7

"RESPECT ME": A CALL FOR CONSENSUAL MARKETING

"A brand is simply trust."
—STEVE JOBS

In our effort to re-establish a business strategy that is "all things human," there is an incredibly large boulder in our path. Technology.

Technology has become the enemy of great marketing.

I know that sounds outrageous because you *love* technology and you're feeling sad right now. Maybe you even want to send me an angry tweet defending the awesomeness of technology and the effectiveness of your "martech stack."

But can I ask you to put that tweet aside for a moment so you can hear me out? Technology isn't bad. In fact, the problem with technology is that it's *so good*. It's so efficient and easy that we tend to assign every marketing problem to a tech solution ... even when we shouldn't. And that's just the beginning of the problem.

There are four ways we're mis-using technology in ways that disrespect our customers.

1. The cycle of annoyance

Last year I noticed a promotion about an interesting study available for free from the Salesforce website. This a great company I've admired and trusted for many years. But I became suspicious when I was required to provide my title, email, and (gasp) phone number in exchange for the document. I was willing to put my trust in one of my favorite companies, and so I complied.

In the next 24 hours I received:

- An unsolicited phone call from a sales representative
- An email from the same sales rep (after I already said I wasn't interested!)
- An invitation to a webinar
- A blog-based newsletter
- An entirely different newsletter from the company relevant to the defense industry, which I have nothing to do with.

I complained to my sales rep about this shower of interruptions and never received a reply. As an experiment, I downloaded another document, and yes, the cycle of annoyance started all over again, beginning with a phone call in the middle of my birthday party.

After this incident, I was so unhappy and distrustful of this company that I wrote a blog post about my experience (which *still* didn't elicit a response).

What a weird turn of events. This premier, Fortune 500 company that I have long-admired used marketing automation to twist a raving fan into a suspicious and annoyed business professional writing a negative blog post to tens of thousands of readers.

This is not just about one company, of course. It's about *every* company that abuses our personal rights and litters our lives with every form of spam. Who wouldn't want to rebel against that?

Simply downloading a pdf doesn't make me a "lead," and it doesn't mean anybody has the right to interrupt my day with calls and emails and newsletters that I never subscribed to.

Marketing, advertising, and PR are lost in a technological fog. We've taken the smartest people and most powerful machines in the history of the world and used them to trick people to click on links or give up an email address.

By comparison, in the medical profession, emerging technology is being used to cure disease and improve life expectancy. In physics, technology helps us discover the origins of the universe and the mysteries of space.

But in my own beloved profession of marketing, the primary application of technology is to find increasingly sophisticated ways to annoy people.

We can do better. We *must* do better, because this exploitation is jet fuel for the Third Rebellion. Say it with me fellow consumers: "I will not be controlled or manipulated. I will not stand for this abuse. I am your customer, but I'm in control. Respect me."

The world is far too competitive to embrace marketing technology that forces people into rebellion. If you're in marketing, be a marketer. Put the customer first, always. Protect the brand. Protect your customers. How did we forget this?

I want to pledge my allegiance to Salesforce, a company that I love. But they marketed the faith right out of me.

This little story is a symptom of the larger disease.

The heart, the soul, the truest pulse of marketing is vaporizing because our profession is turning into a glorified IT function. Marketing strategy is being derived from data scientists, SEO gurus, and statisticians doing A/B testing in a back room somewhere. It's time to take it back.

2. Just because you *can* doesn't mean you *should*.

I'm not anti-technology or anti-data. In fact, I'm a data geek. There is absolutely an important place for all these functions in the marketing universe if we can use technology to *be more human.* Done well, marketing automation is invisible and in service of the customer. But we cross the line when we implement tactics based on what is statistically supposed to work instead of what we know customers really want.

Here's an example: pop-up ads.

Every research report concludes that consumers LOATHE pop-up ads.[48] And while pop-ups might slightly increase sign-up rates for a newsletter, at this point, there's no rational marketing professional who can believe that people like these maddening interruptions.

But if you ask a marketer why they do it, they say "because they work."

But people hate them.

But they work.

And so it goes.

In 2014, Ethan Zuckerman, the inventor of the pop-up ad, wrote a lengthy apology for his creation in *The Atlantic*. He called it "The Internet's Original Sin" and pleaded with businesses to "ditch them."

Another example of tech gone wrong is the popular practice of *lead nurturing*, which is just a pleasant way to say, "I'm going to keep barraging you with emails until you block me." But when everybody does it, the practice seems okay. We do it because we're afraid *not* to do it.

Why are we are abusing and disrespecting our customers at every turn? Here are some more examples:

- Many smart TVs include software that tracks what you watch and sends your viewing habits back to the home office. Privacy advocates worry that viewers – seniors in particular – are being left in the dark by click-through agreements and complicated privacy settings. Should we have to even worry about the privacy setting on our TV?

- Robo-calls, which are increasing every year, now utilize technology to trick regulators by making the call origins impossible to trace. One tactic known as "neighborhood spoofing" fools people by using fake local numbers in the hope that recipients will be more likely to pick up. Conning customers is a marketing strategy?

- Advertisers are finding creative ways around ad blockers on our smart devices in a sort of counter-attack against the rebellion. They're penalizing people who self-selected to block ads – which implies they don't want to see ads – by forcing them to watch *more* ads. Does that make any sense?

- The cost of email marketing is so low that even one response may justify the expense. The efficiency of the tech actually encourages marketers to abuse it. One person explained this to me: "We're expected to blast pitches because one out of a million will actually respond. Maybe we get lucky and it hits them with the right message at the right time." True, but you're also spamming 999,999 people in the process!

This situation seems strangely familiar. Didn't all of our problems start a hundred years ago because competition forced marketers on a race to the bottom? Here we go again.

And the problem is bound to get worse. Forrester predicts CMOs will spend more than $122 billion on marketing automation, adtech, and database services by 2022. But studies show that just 28 percent feel they have the internal talent to actually manage the technology they already have.[49]

I'm fearful that access to Minority Report-style facial recognition, wearable tracking devices, and human-like chatbots will unleash a new wave of marketing creepiness. I'm afraid that we're in an industry on the cusp of creating hate at scale.

3. Technology is not the "easy button."

When I was the marketing director for a global packaging business, we systematically travelled the world each year to see our customers face-to-face. In this breathtaking universe of technology and online surveys, that might seem incredibly wasteful until you realize this practice saved our company.

My colleague and I were finishing up our tenth customer visit over a period of two months. We had learned a lot, but it had been an exhausting exercise and we were glad to be near the end and heading home.

In the last moments of our last interview, a packaging scientist from a major soft drink company made an offhand remark as we were packing up: "By the way, did you see this new government research that came out about Chemical XYZ? The FDA apparently has found something that indicates it might be a health hazard."

We were stunned. We had not heard about this. Indeed, it was a preliminary report from an obscure department – almost nobody had heard about it.

My colleague, a technical leader for our company, investigated and found that the new research was far from conclusive and years from being validated ... but it was real enough that we needed to find a replacement coating for our products. Changing food packaging is a glacial process that takes years of testing and millions of dollars of development. More than one person in our company questioned why we were changing a chemical when we were already obeying all the laws.

Five years later, the research had been completed and the bombastic findings made the front page of *The Wall Street Journal.* By that time, the chemical had already been eliminated from all of our packaging, years in advance. The tip we received from a customer had literally saved our company and our customers.

The notable point here is that we never would have had this breakthrough if we were only connecting to our customers through an online survey or a customer chat function. No matter how great our online "listening" software might have been, that vital insight never would have shown up on a social media dashboard or the comment section of a blog.

We know this human connection is irreplaceable, and yet we're on an inexorable march toward the mythical marketing easy button that tries to eliminate humans from our customer processes. Technology has made us lazy and lethargic.

"I was doing a speech at the World Business Forum in New York just a year ago," said marketing consultant Martin Lindstrom. "I had 5,000 people in the audience and I asked, 'How many people have spent time sitting down with a consumer in the last year?' Twenty people raised a hand. Out of 5,000! This is the major problem we have in marketing today."

4. The uninvited guest

When people complain that "marketing ruins everything," more often than not they're really condemning the programmatic ads that interrupt them, the deluge of spammy emails, the direct mail that clutters their mailbox, and the endlessly irritating phone messages from robo-callers. While the functions of marketing and advertising are distinct (I actually regard advertising as a subset of marketing) in the consumer's view, it's all the same.

If I'm providing a path for a human-centered and values-based approach to marketing, discussing the dark side state of automation, digital advertising, and marketing technology is unavoidable.

Earlier in the book I suggest that we're inevitably moving toward an ad-free world ... and that's true in the sense that most people would feel liberated from those annoying intrusions. The world has been rebelling against irrelevant and invasive ads for 100 years. But for the time being, advertising and marketing dollars subsidize nearly the entire internet. Without ads, many valuable companies like Google and Facebook would be doomed.

In 1994, two university scholars wrote an article for *The Journal of Advertising* titled, "The Death of Advertising." Since then, the industry has doubled in size. So it would be really stupid of me to say that advertising is dead. I'm not going to be that guy, and please don't tweet that either. At least for now, advertising is essential to the world economy, and the model can't be replaced in the foreseeable future.

Worldwide, marketing is a $1 trillion industry and growing. The global advertising spend typically rises about 3 percent to 4 percent each year, which makes me wonder – if we *know* that most people don't see our ads or trust them, *where's all this money going?*

Of course, most of this advertising investment is moving to the digital realm. The ease of creating and posting a digital ad through Facebook or Google means that more organizations run ads today than any other time in history. Anybody with a budget over $10 can take out an ad that is precise, immediate, and measurable.

So why aren't "targeted online ads" the simple answer to all our problems and the end of this book? Because online advertising, our great hope, is also the most ignored advertising form ever created. It's not unusual for an ad with 100,000 impressions to never be clicked. (Perhaps that's because many of the ads we see are for items we've already purchased!)

Like the media industry it has long subsidized, digital advertising is convulsed by change.

"In the early days of online media, the choice was essentially made – give it away for free, and advertising would produce the revenue," said Randall Rothenberg, chief executive of the Interactive Advertising Bureau. "A lot of the problems we see now flow out from that decision."[50]

Rothenberg's organization has long pushed for stronger standards for online advertising. In a speech, he implored the industry to "take civic responsibility for our effect on the world." But he conceded the business was growing and changing too quickly for many to comprehend its ethical dilemmas and excesses, let alone fix them.

"Technology has been outpacing the ability of individual companies to understand what is actually going on," he said.

How do we get out of this cycle?

Thankfully, there's a growing chorus of respected professional voices who are fed up with the marketing industry's abuse of tech. Renowned technology journalist Walt Mossberg called for reform:

"Too often, poorly executed, annoying, code-heavy, privacy-invading ads clutter websites and apps ... Videos are abandoned because of pre-roll ads that are too long or too boring. Users go crazy trying to silence auto-playing video ads.

"Programmatic ads, automatically placed by Google and others, are especially junky and repetitive. Publishers have little control over them. Native ads – in which advertiser-written articles or videos are intermingled with standard content – are too hard to distinguish from editorial matter.

"If the industry doesn't change, and fast, consumers will do it for us."

In a TED talk, author and futurist Jaron Lanier said the industry is on a knife's edge and referred to Facebook and Google advertising practices as "behavior modification empires."

Ev Williams, former CEO of Twitter and founder of the long-form content site Medium, denounced the corrupt ad model in a personal post: "It's clear that the broken system is ad-driven media on the internet. It simply doesn't serve people. In fact, it's not designed to. The vast majority of articles, videos, and other content we all consume on a daily basis is paid for – directly or indirectly – by corporations who are funding it to advance their goals. And content is measured, amplified, and rewarded based on its ability to do that. Period. As a result, we get ... well, what we get. And it's getting worse."

As a solution, Ev ended the advertising model on Medium and is trying to make a go of it with a subscription model. (I was among the first to sign-up, and I hope you will, too!)

Ironically, these problems have not been caused by any technological disruption, shift in consumer behavior, or misguided government regulations. We've brought these problems on ourselves.

Marketers are too often directed by short-term algorithmic impulses instead of building trust and establishing a fair value exchange with consumers.

Dr. Kotler's lesson that marketing is "all things human" seems like a faraway memory.

CONSENSUAL MARKETING

"There's going to be a seismic shift in the agency world," predicted Josh Dean, the CMO of fashion brand Tommy John. "Everything is programmed and automated and we don't even have a good sense of what's happening or where the money is going. We have forgotten the human connection, the human component. We need to have consensual marketing."

Marketing to the digital natives has to be consensual: We agree to give something up (our data, our feedback, our money) in exchange for a commensurate good or service. But through widespread use of marketing automation, the balance of power has moved from the customers to the advertisers collecting the data. The value exchange is usually nonexistent.

"Today, the customer journey sometimes seems like an ant farm," said Megan Conley, founder and CEO of Social Tribe. "Businesses want us to run through these prescribed pathways designed without my consent. It feels like somebody is trying to control or manipulate my behavior. It's a question of my choice, of opting-in, of free will. I don't think consumers are anti-loyalty, but they do want to consent. We want to be respected. Businesses need to design the conditions where each phase of the customer journey is co-created with the customer. That's the shift needed in marketing today.

"In the earliest days of marketing, we saw an ad or a billboard and we had no choice and we couldn't interact with it. With social media, that wall came down. Now, customers who were talking about our products and brands tried to join in, but it was after the fact, after the product had been purchased.

"I think the third frontier is making your customer a partner in how you build your brand and how you build your product, even shaping the future of your business, and that becomes the new customer journey."

We must come to some accommodation. How can marketing technology and our human customers peacefully coexist and thrive together?

BURNING THROUGH TRUST

Prolific marketing guru Seth Godin remarked that the current advertising ecosystem is making companies "burn through trust." He wrote:

"There's an uncanny valley here, that uncomfortable feeling we get when we know we're being played, when someone mass customizes and tries to steal the value of actual person-to-person connection.

"It's a trap because the more you do it, the more you need to do it. Once you start burning trust, the only way to keep up is to burn more trust ... it's a bit like throwing the walls of your house in the fireplace to stay warm.

"Don't waste your time and money on this. You're wasting the most valuable thing you own – trust."

Humanity is too valuable to try to steal with your robo-calling software.

The thought that troubles me is that in today's environment, "trust" is actually a point of differentiation. Doesn't that seem bizarre? Especially when we *know* that trust IS the brand! And yet companies seem so willing to give it up when they're in the invisible grasp of the marketing technology black hole.

COME ALONGSIDE YOUR CUSTOMER

Getting out of this rut will take extraordinary leadership. Somebody at the top of your organization has to put their foot down and declare that the *trust will not be broken.* Trust becomes the dominant strategic lens.

One of the most dramatic examples of a cultural adjustment to these consumer realities can be found at Microsoft. There's no such thing as a grassroots cultural change. It has to come from the leader, as exemplified by the company's CEO Satya Nadella. In his excellent book, *Hit Refresh,* Satya links the lessons and culture of his childhood in India to a dramatic cultural refresh at one of the world's largest companies. This human-centered approach touches every aspect of life at Microsoft, from HR policies to investment decisions.

I had a chance to sit down with Amit Panchal, Microsoft's director of competitive strategy, to ask him how moving from a tech-oriented culture to a human-centered culture is reflected in the company's sales and marketing approach.

"Let's be honest," he said, "back in the old days, sales people at Microsoft and the customer were dating. We sold you software and we more or less walked away. The goal was the sale. If you used our product, great, if not, no problem. And then a few years later we would come back at contract time and ask you to sign on the dotted line.

"But we never asked the question, 'Do you find value in the tools you are using?' Did customers get any value out of it?

"Now, those questions are at the center of what we do. We want to come alongside our customers in a collaborative partnership. If they're not fully using the products they buy, we are both failing.

"The key issue is not 'will they buy more?' but 'how can our customers achieve more with what they have?' Our measurement of success is our customer success. That might seem old-fashioned, but when you think about it, this drives new behaviors in marketing, the correct behaviors in marketing – kinder and gentler approaches. Coming alongside customers isn't going to happen from some special use of marketing automation. It's going to come from getting out there and listening to people. Are you learning the customer's business? Do you understand what's in their pipeline? Who is challenging them? Who is destroying them?

"Marketing success can't be simply measured by financial gain any more. It has to be measured by your *customer's* financial gain."

TECHNOLOGY CAN EASE THE CUSTOMER JOURNEY

I'd like to build on Amit's view of how we should come alongside our customers and break the cycle of abusive technology. Customers rarely fit into the traditional sales pipeline anymore. They're on their own journey of discovery, which means we need to be constantly in front of them.

The McKinsey researchers who first codified this principle and discovered that two-thirds of our marketing is being driven by customer-generated activities also showed that the best use of technology is not to intercept or interrupt but rather to make the consumer's path to our products fast and easy.[51]

We can win when we use technology to make the sales process transparent and compassionate, leading customers to trust us and rely on us. The best marketing technology should:

- Streamline the customer journey (online banking is a good example of this)

- Personalize and optimize customer experiences along the journey

- Proactively provide customer service (like a site that texts your order status)

- Provide delight by using customer information to predict needs and respond with relevant products and services (like an airline app that allows you to have ground transportation waiting for you)

HUMANITY THROUGH TECHNOLOGY?

Technology can ease the customer journey, but is it also possible to use something like artificial intelligence to make our companies more human? How can we use technology to actually *build trust*?

There's no better person to answer the question than Christopher S. Penn, co-founder and CEO of Trust Insights. Chris is sort of a marketing Yoda. He understands complex technology but can explain it in movie-quality sound bites. He offered to riff on the bright side of emerging technology and how it will help us build a more human company:

"It's important to establish upfront that technology is simply a utensil. It's not going to do magic by itself; it still needs humans behind the steering wheel.

"The Artificial Intelligence utensil does three things very well: acceleration, accuracy, and automation. And this is where AI really shines for marketers. It means data processing that is much faster, much better, much cleaner ... it means getting to conclusions faster, it means understanding attribution much faster. And so, a lot of our marketing processes like analysis, predictive analytics, and forecasting will just become much easier and take up less time.

"AI isn't human. Not even close. It's statistics. It's probability. It can look at a photo of a hot dog and determine that yes, this is probably a hot dog – a yes or no kind of decision.

"Now, how does this apply to making our marketing more human? Well, if you're spending all your time copying and pasting from one spreadsheet to another – which I have seen people do in marketing and PR agencies – you're going to immediately free up time to do human things like talking to prospective customers, attending networking events, doing truly creative work.

"I think we will see humanity resurface in our work because we'll have insights we never had before. Think about all the decades of data you might have in your call center or CRM database. All these technologies will help us understand thousands or millions of conversations and interactions at scale.

"Think about the pile of reviews a company might have on Yelp or other review sites. Who has time to analyze 20,000 reviews ... and competitor reviews? Machine learning can help us do that.

"Most companies have many decades of data essentially locked away. Perhaps with AI we can truly tune in to our customers like never before. That makes your marketing and your business, frankly, more human.

"Truth is embedded in that data. AI can help us dissect and sort and analyze those known quantities. But humans are best at discovering the unknown quantities, the insights that can really grow our business. Those unknowns might be discovered through focus groups, conferences, networking events, coffee, breakfast, dinner, drinks at the bar, and wherever you learn from humans. AI gives us that time to explore and focus on the humanity because the human stuff doesn't scale. Machines are not going to be able to channel empathy, ethics, judgment, or aggregate life experiences any time soon. They won't be able to discern new landmines ahead for our businesses.

"There is also a possibility that AI can be used in a company to be more human than your humans. This is a tricky one, but it's important for businesses and marketers to hear. If the customer experience with your brand is so awful that people would rather deal with a machine, then AI is going to improve your brand by cutting the people out. Even if AI is mediocre, that's better than awful. And at least it's a stable and standardized mediocre! Over time, AI can be 'trained' to model our very best human service practices and it will never be irritable, tired, or worn down by the drudgery of repetitive tasks."

PEACE AND PROFITS THROUGH TECH

I first met Baratunde Thurston at the annual SXSW conference, and he has become one of my favorite writers, lecturers, and humorists. To help lead us into a world where humans come first, he created an open-source document on Google called the "New Tech Manifesto."[52] He started the conversation in a blog post and asked the world to contribute guidelines that can be adopted for a more human-centered approach to marketing technology, data collection, and privacy.

I agree with Baratunde that a human-centered marketing revolution can't rise from individual actions. The more likely source of change will come if one business at a time begins to adopt guidelines pledging openness and honesty with our marketing technology practices. Here are some ideas to build trust through technology:

1. Offer real transparency around data collection and usage.

Real transparency means we should be able to see how our data is being used as easily as we can discover that someone "liked" our post. We should understand what's inside the tech products we use without having to read novel-length legal documents. And we deserve to know clearly and upfront what companies are doing with our data, including how they are monetizing it – even if they're not selling the raw data itself.

Companies could take a cue from the food industry, which is required by the federal government to include standard nutrition labels on products. Imagine something like a data usage label or scorecard that demystifies the terms of service and allows users to see what's being tracked.

2. Change data defaults from open to closed.

We sign up for a service and trust that the people who made it aren't trying to rob us (and who has time to flip through all those settings, anyway?). But they are, metaphorically, out to rob us. Defaults matter.

Most tech products grab as much data from as many users as possible regardless of whether that data is currently useful. But in most cases, companies don't need all that data in order to provide their services. What if they flipped the defaults?

What if the data extraction defaults were as constrained as possible?

3. Respect our right to our own data.

Baratunde's manifesto proposes that we extend property rights to cover our data – both the data we *generate* (like photos or tweets) and data *derived from our activities* (like our purchase history, location, swipes, taps, and clicks).

Without our data, these services wouldn't have anything to monetize. Without our data, the artificial-intelligence systems powering machine vision, speech recognition, and many other technologies of the future would be blind.

When you understand that it is our user-generated data powering the foundations of future innovation and wealth, we become more than users. We become partners with rights to determine how our contributions are used. The exchange must be consensual.

4. Implement new laws.

Most people cringe when considering "technology" and "regulation" in the same sentence. But it's time – past time – for leaders in the tech space to encourage regulation. In the U.S., legislators have demonstrated that they don't know enough about the tech landscape to even ask the right questions, let alone deliver and enforce effective new laws. Ironically, the ideas behind new regulations may have to come from tech industry leaders.

As we witnessed in the First Rebellion, the marketing/ad/ tech industry cannot regulate itself. Government had to step in to end the lies. Eventually, it will have to step in once again to place ethical boundaries on technology and protect us.

5. Build trust into everything we do.

The primary problem with marketing technology is that we're trading trust for expediency. Marketers must rise up and become defenders of our customers instead of the epicenters of spam.

Lisa Wood, CMO at Atom Bank, is a great example of this. "Our aim is to do what is best for customers and build from the customer out," she said. "Trust is absolutely embedded into our marketing strategy and built into the culture of the company. Transparency is one of our design standards, one of the things we hold ourselves accountable to when designing our value proposition."[53]

Nine in 10 consumers are more willing to give transparent brands a second chance after a bad experience or company crisis. This is a simple idea. We can build trust in our companies by being honest about how we're using technology and consumer data.

ARE YOU IN?

I want to believe that people will read this chapter and say, "Yes! It's about time somebody said this!" But I know many will also respond with "but Mark, there is no bad technology. Only bad marketers."

That's not necessarily true. The marketer and the application of the technology represents a system. The marketer can be defined by the technology. The technology can be defined by the marketer. It's symbiotic.

So how do we wrestle technology to the ground and make it serve the constant human truths? It's a complicated problem.

We're not going to slow the race toward AI everything. We're not going to eliminate lazy marketing or the quixotic search for the marketing easy button.

The answer to the problem isn't in a database.

The answer is certainly not in a pop-up ad.

But the answer might reside in the answer to a simple question: *What do our customers love?*

Now, use your technology to do exactly that.

PART THREE

REACHING THE UNREACHABLE

CHAPTER 8

A MANIFESTO FOR HUMAN-CENTERED MARKETING

Now that I've explored the constant human truths and their connection to business success, I thought I'd summarize some of the key lessons in the form of guidelines that lead to more human-centered marketing. If you visit businessesGROW.com/rebellion, you can find a high-quality copy of these lessons you can print-out.

A MANIFESTO FOR HUMAN-CENTERED MARKETING

1. Stop doing what customers hate. Get out there and discover what customers love. Do that (at least).

2. Technology should be invisible to your customer and only used to help your company be more compassionate, receptive, fascinating, and useful.

3. You can't "own" customers, a buyer's journey, or a sales funnel. Claim a market space and help people belong to it.

4. Never intercept, never interrupt. Earn the invitation.

5. Be relevant, consistent, and superior. Build trust into everything you do.

6. Be fans of your fans. Make them the heroes of your story.

7. Transcend the public's inherent mistrust of your company through relentless honesty.

8. Don't be "in" the customer community. Be "of" the customer community.

9. Marketing is never about your "why." It's about your customer's "why."

10. The most human company wins.

CHAPTER 9

YOUR CUSTOMERS ARE YOUR MARKETERS

*"If you talked to people the way advertising
talked to people, they'd punch you in the face."*
—HUGH MACLEOD

Recently I vacationed in the stunning Cycladic Islands of Greece. It was an exhilarating trip to the cradle of civilization.

It also inspired a marketing lesson. Of course. I am so weird that way.

All 220 islands were formed by volcanic activity millions of years ago and have similar landscapes, vegetation, and climate. They're so close together that you can see neighboring islands from any ocean vista.

And yet, they are all so different! Over the years, each tiny island developed its own microculture of food, art, history, customs, and stories that are endless sources of local pride. No matter where you turn, everybody knows each other and they're all chatting, waving, and laughing. Who knew you could visit the 20 most-inhabited islands in this chain and find 20 fascinating microcultures?

And that is a metaphor for our modern marketing world.

THE LIKE-MINDED ISLANDS

Technology has allowed our customers to self-organize into like-minded islands. (Futurist Faith Popcorn calls this "micro-clanning.") The consumer islands are unique places of respect, conversation, and community populated by friends, families, trusted experts, and maybe even a few visitors known as *influencers*.

Like inhabitants of any small island, communication travels quickly, and there is a strong shared history, bonds of trust, and wariness of strangers. For fun, most people travel back and forth to nearby islands to visit tribes of friends with other shared interests.

Naturally, businesses are desperate to be invited to these clannish consumer islands. They are convinced the islanders would buy their goods and services if they would only give them a chance.

In the days before the like-minded islands, businesses embraced mass marketing. Unwanted mail. Endless email blasts. Repetitive ads.

Now that the islanders have seized control and can determine who can enter their island, those tactics don't work anymore. Who would want that aggravation?

In fact, these clever islanders have even developed technology to block and drown out every unwanted interruption. Some of the "messaging" still leaks through, but it's only a matter of time before people figure out how to live their peaceful island lives without annoyances from bothersome marketers. And so, the islanders have become increasingly isolated and unreachable.

What should a business do? Some still cling to advertising and the old ways. It's familiar and easy to fly over the island with a banner ad, hoping somebody will look up and notice. But things are far too busy and interesting on the island for anybody to care.

ASK THE ISLANDERS

What if we asked the islanders what our businesses would have to do to become invited to the like-minded island? What would they tell us? It might be something like:

- Be a friend. Fit in and belong. Do something useful.

- Respect our time, our freedom, and our privacy.

- Come alongside us and be there when we need you.

- Show us that you share our values, even if it makes you unpopular on other islands. If we're going to be loyal to you, you have to be loyal to us.

- Create fun experiences that show us what life is like beyond our limited view of this island.

- Don't just tell us you're great and you belong here. We want to see it – here and now on this island. That's the only thing we'll believe.

- Never annoy us or show up uninvited. That's just rude.

This is a pretty rational and realistic perspective, isn't it? It suggests a human-centered approach to marketing more in line with constant human values and truths.

Here's a magical and glorious reality: If you're ever invited to an island, your "marketing" can stop! Yes, the islanders can be protective and selfish, but if they trust and love you, they're also generous. When you belong, the islanders do the marketing for you. They tell their family and friends how cool and helpful you are. They're seen around the island hanging out with you. You're part of their daily routine. The islanders stick with you and fight for you even if you're attacked by competitors.

In this new consumer world, we're no longer in control of any sales funnel or customer journey. The best we can hope for is to be part of an ongoing conversation that leads to an invitation to an island.

ISLAND TACTICS

I've covered some high-level ideas in this book. Now, let's look at specific tactics that can help you connect with the digital islanders and influence that two-thirds of marketing that is going on without you.

The purpose of this chapter is *not* to be a comprehensive how-to guide – that would fill another five books, and there's plenty about these topics for you to access online. Instead, I'll provide a summary of 15 "human-centered marketing" tactics that should serve your islanders well.

CUSTOMER EXPERIENCE

A recent survey of CEOs named customer experience as the top priority for chief marketing officers, and for good reason.[54] It's a virtuous cycle: Customers fall in love with what you're doing and stir up buzz about it. The buzz leads to consideration from the shop-around buyers.

The key strategy is to build an emotional connection into your user experience and every customer touchpoint. Let's look at how the online music service Spotify does this.

Like many software-as-a-service companies, Spotify offers a "freemium" version of their product with ads every 30 minutes. The goal of this model is to hook customers so they eventually buy an ad-free subscription with cool bonus features.

Let's compare Spotify's conversion rate with other popular freemium software, Dropbox and Evernote – two products I use every day:[55]

Spotify   *27%*

Evernote   *4%*

Dropbox   *4%*

In this business, a 1 percent conversion rate is considered good. A 27 percent conversion rate is ridiculous. Spotify does a lot of things right, but one of the best is how the app helps customers create an emotional connection to their personalized programming.

Spotify uses machine learning to predict the music you want to hear, when you want to hear it. The service uncannily predicts new music you would like and can even spin tunes it believes you probably liked as a kid.

A core reason people listen to music is to intensify a mood. Spotify becomes the soundtrack of your life through their hyper-focused playlists. While I was writing this book, Spotify suggested a playlist for me called "Intense Studying." Right on.

That's a good example of using technology in a smart way to build an emotional connection to a product that lasts.

Another example of building emotion through user experience is the turnaround at the Denver International Airport. When the colossal facility opened in 1995, it was generally regarded as the worst airport in America. It was isolated and expensive, and its baggage handling system was ... mysterious, to say the least.

Seven years ago, Denver's airport management shifted its approach from focusing on airlines to focusing on the passenger experience. That meant investing several million dollars in a faster Wi-Fi system, adding 10,000 electrical charging outlets at seats, recruiting stores and restaurants, establishing rooms for nursing mothers, and speeding up TSA checkpoints. The airport built a public plaza that has a free pop-up skating rink in the winter and a free 18-hole miniature golf course in the summer. (You can borrow complimentary skates and putters.)

"A happy passenger spends more money," said airport CEO Kim Day. Per-passenger spending grew from $10.82 in 2013 to $12.37 in 2017. The added revenue reduces charges to airlines, making it more attractive for carriers to fly to Denver.[56]

In 2018, the airport was named the best airport in the country by *The Wall Street Journal*.

Another incredibly important aspect of customer experience is service. Poor customer service interactions obviously have an adverse effect on brand loyalty: Research shows three-quarters of consumers say poor customer service makes them less likely to purchase products from a brand they're otherwise loyal to. That tops all other factors that would cause people to drop their consideration of a brand.

Brands must deliver experiences that are fast and frictionless. Powerful word-of-mouth content is normally generated during and right after a sale. How can your customer experience provide opportunities for customers to tell your story?

USER-GENERATED CONTENT

In Chapter 3, I covered the idea of unleashing employee-generated content (EGC), and a more common idea is UGC, or *user-generated content.*

User-generated content simply means people authentically and honestly posting about their love of your product. A photo on Instagram, a blog post, and a Facebook Live event at your hotel or conference can represent authentic advocacy. *AdWeek* called the power of human-generated content "social media's most significant contribution to the world of marketing." Research shows:[57]

- Social campaigns that incorporate UGC see a 50 percent lift in engagement.

- Ads featuring UGC generate five times greater click-through rates.

- 90 percent of respondents in a survey said UGC influenced their online purchases, a higher percentage than search engine results, email marketing, ads, or company social media posts.

This success has naturally caught the attention of the marketing technology world, and there are numerous platforms available to help you discover, curate, and even generate UGC. However, any company can roll up its sleeves and generate customer buzz, so consider these tactics:

1. A customer's delight is at its highest peak right when they buy a product. Tap into that emotion and encourage customers to take action with social media posts at the point of purchase.

2. According to Netsphere Strategies, 63 percent of U.S. customers and 66 percent of U.K. shoppers trust customer product photos more than brand or retailer photos. One of the simplest strategies for your business is to encourage visual testimonials at the second point of delight – right after they've received their product.

3. Give customers a reason to engage with the brand. I encourage my customers to create "Instagram moments," which are powerful, fun, or amazing visual elements in the customer environment. New Jersey orthodontist Tara Gostovich literally rolls out a red carpet for teens who have their braces removed. She gives them a crown or tiara, balloons, and cool sunglasses as the staff snaps photos that are sent to the parent's smartphone. If you have a giant inflated anything (doughnut, gorilla, puppy), people will stand in front of it and share it with friends.

4. Authors Jay Baer and Daniel Lemin wrote an excellent book called *Talk Triggers* filled with logical, accessible strategies focused on optimizing empathy, usefulness, generosity, speed, and attitude to enable shareable moments. These conversation triggers can be as simple as warm cookies at a Doubletree Hotel or hilarious hold music for a conference calling service.

The best way to encourage UGC is to get in front of customers and make something post-worthy happen. Sarah Nunes, director of brand communications at Vistaprint, and her team members traveled around the country for six months in a branded RV to meet with customers and provide an opportunity to create content about her company.

"We love seeing the amazing images that our customers post of our products," she said. "and we make sure to share them back out whenever we can on our social networks and website. Not only do we recognize their appreciation, we also help market their businesses through our channels. When other customers see that, it motivates them to post their own images, creating broader marketing for us."[58]

WORD-OF-MOUTH MARKETING

Word-of-mouth marketing (WOMM) is the oldest way to promote a product, and it still can be the most effective. In a world where most people have their heads down in a screen, hearing a product recommendation from a real live person carries a lot of weight.

The numbers are too big to ignore. On average we spend 30 percent of our day in conversation, and 15 percent of those conversations refer to a brand or product.[59] What can you do to seed your stories into those conversations?

Despite the obvious business case for WOMM, it's an underutilized technique because it requires patience and hard work. You can't automate it, you can't algorithm it, and you certainly can't push the marketing easy button. You have to show up on the customer islands and make these conversations happen.

WOMM practice and theory rests on pioneering measurement techniques established by Ed Keller and his team at Engagement Lab. They discovered that about 10 percent of the population are *super sharers* who organize their lives to talk about cool new things they've discovered. If you can put something extraordinary and relevant in front of them, they'll do the rest of the work and carry your story far and wide.

Here's the basic WOMM strategy:

1. Through insight and research, establish stories about your company or product that are authentic, interesting, relevant, and repeatable.

2. Connect those stories to ideal focus audiences who will share your stories organically as opportunities arise.

3. Build a competency in continuously and effectively sharing this story in face-to-face settings, perhaps through creative activations, and train others to do so.

In an era of fake news and toxic social media streams, this old-school technique is finding new life. Keller found that 19 percent of consumer purchases in the U.S. are caused by word-of-mouth conversations, both online and offline.[60]

Some of the case studies I've mentioned in this book, including Room & Board, Lululemon, and YETI coolers, depended almost entirely on word-of-mouth marketing over traditional advertising, marketing, and PR.

Aliza Freud is a former vice president of global marketing and brand management for American Express, and she's now CEO of SheSpeaks, a market research firm. She relies entirely on word-of-mouth marketing to spread news about her research and clients.

"Consumers have the authenticity and voice that is trusted by the audience you want to reach," she said. "You have to allow the customer to have the flexibility and creative control in telling a benefit-driven story. As marketers, we frequently get caught up in the features of our products. But at the end of the day, that consumer only cares about how relevant you are to making their life better, easier, more interesting, and exciting. If a consumer can articulate how your product is a real benefit in their lives, then you have a great story."[61]

Emily Weiss, CEO of Glossier (profiled in Chapter 10), turned her fashion blog into a multi-million-dollar millennial makeup empire entirely through word-of-mouth marketing.

Emily attributes her company's explosive growth and cultural clout to its hyper-engaged fanbase: an army of Glossier girls who follow the brand's every product announcement, Instagram post, interview, and event invitation. They amplify the brand's message to their followers on social media and in real life. She estimates that Glossier owes 90 percent of its revenue to these fans.

In the Glossier world, cosmetics aren't just products – they're content. Emily sees every new creation as an opportunity to ignite customer conversations.[62]

The idea of building "talkability" into products and events is also known as creating the "social object" that can be carried forward by your best fans.

Hugh MacLeod of Gapingvoid explained, "We're all naturally enthusiastic about something outside ourselves. For me, it's marketing and cartooning. For others, it could be cellphones or Scotch whisky or Apple computers or NASCAR or the Boston Red Sox. All these act as social objects within a network of people who care passionately about their stuff. Whatever industry you are in, there's somebody who is geeked out about your product category. They're using your product (or a competitor's product) as a social object. If you don't understand how the geeks are socializing – connecting to other people – via your product, then you don't actually have a marketing plan. Heck, you probably don't have a viable business plan."[63]

One of the themes in this book is the need for marketers to close out of their digital dashboards and get out and talk to customers. Discovering how customers are already sharing your stories can help you formulate a WOMM strategy for your own business.

Be sure to discover the valuable free Word of Mouth Marketing workbook at www.businessesGROW.com/rebellion.

PEER OBSERVATION

Researchers from the Cranfield School of Management[64] discovered that observing what your friends are buying is a common way to make purchasing decisions, shape views of a brand, and provide a psychological influence at least equal to word-of-mouth product recommendations.

It makes sense. With so many decisions to make in our lives, it saves effort to assume that if others are using a product, we're making a decent bet if we do the same thing.

The researchers point to four practical strategies to enable peer observations:

- **Use distinctive branding.** A notable identity can help us distinguish what product is being used. An example is Apple's signature white ear buds – we know it's Apple even when we can't see the device. Another example is the unique, branded glass you receive when served a pint of Guinness beer. You can recognize a pint of Guinness even in a dimly lit pub!

- **Appeal to groups.** Offering group discounts or specials can win the group and reinforce that the purchasing decision is accepted by friends.

- **Expose normally invisible customer behaviors to peers.** On a website, adding counts and statistics of how many people are buying increases both sales and the price customers will pay. And if the figures are from *my group* that is buying, so much the better.

- **Build peer observation into product launches.** Hutchison launched its social media-enabled mobile handset INQ in Singapore by hiring a tribe of young people to use the bright, colorful handsets while walking around crowded transit stations. If you identify with the group, you may identify with the product.

THE PEAK MOMENTS

One of the best ways to generate post-sales buzz is by engineering shareable moments into your customer's experience. In their excellent book, *The Power of Moments,* researchers Chip and Dan Heath demonstrate that customers easily forgive mistakes along the way if you provide them with memorable peak experiences they can share with others.

Consider the Magic Castle Hotel, one of the top-rated properties in Los Angeles according to TripAdvisor, just ahead of the iconic Hotel Bel-Air. Out of more than 3,000 reviews, 94 percent rate the hotel as either "excellent" or "very good."[65]

There's a puzzle behind the hotel's ranking, though. If you scan the photos of the resort online, you would never conclude, "That's one of the best hotels in L.A." The pool is small, the rooms are dated, the furnishings are sparse, and most walls are bare. In fact, even the word "hotel" seems like a stretch – the Magic Castle is a converted two-story apartment complex from the 1950s, painted yellow. It looks like a respectable budget motel. How could it be one of the best hotels in L.A.?

Let's start with the cherry red phone mounted near the pool. You pick it up and someone answers, "Hello, Popsicle Hotline." You place an order, and minutes later, a staffer wearing white gloves delivers your cherry, orange, or grape popsicles to you poolside. On a silver tray. For free.

Then there's the Snack Menu, a list of goodies ranging from Kit-Kats to Cheetos that can be ordered at no cost. There's also a Board Game Menu and a DVD Menu, with all items loaned for free. Three times a week, magicians perform tricks at breakfast. Did I mention you can drop off unlimited loads of laundry for free washing?

What the Magic Castle figured out is that delighting customers doesn't mean obsessing over every detail. Customers will forgive small swimming pools and underwhelming décor as long as you deliver a few magical peak moments.

What if we mindfully create for our customers peak experiences that generate positive reviews and customer conversations?

Elevated moments have three characteristics that you can consider for your own business:

- Turn up the volume on sensory appeal. Things that look better, taste better, sound better, or feel better usually *are* better.

- Raise the stakes. Add an element of productive pressure, such as a competition, a game, a performance, a deadline, or a public commitment. Deliberately try to "up the ante." We feel most comfortable when things are certain, but we feel most alive when they're not.

- Break the script and violate expectations about an experience. The popsicle menu. The Hyatt hotel hug. Giving away cool, free stuff in your book (wink)!

One simple diagnostic to gauge whether you've transcended the ordinary is if people feel the need to pull out their cameras. If they take pictures, it must be special. That's the moment of elevation that creates conversations.

The Heaths found that the peak experiences *within* a customer engagement and at the *last* moment are especially important. They cite research at a Disney theme park, when they asked customers to rate their satisfaction at each hour of the day on a scale from 1 to 10. For example, hour one when you're paying high prices for tickets might be rated a 2. The second hour might be rated a 3 because you're waiting in line for a ride. Hour three is a 10 because your kids meet Mickey Mouse ... and so on. The last hour of the day – the parade and fireworks display – was nearly always rated a 9 or 10.

If you average the rating of all the hours, it's typically a 6. But on customer surveys, people rated the experience of the entire day as a 9 because they remember the peak experience and the last experience and forget the disappointments in between.

This is a powerful insight to build connection with your own customers. In your company, who has the job of creating peak experiences? Or perhaps a better question is, who will shoot down your ideas because you can't explain the ROI of an orange popsicle?

PSYCHOLOGICAL OWNERSHIP

The simple concept of *psychological ownership* helps explain the appeal of what I describe as artisanal marketing – consumers feel so invested in a product that it becomes an extension of their identities.

A tech company I work with provides its best customers with early access to new product features and designs. They involve their customers in creating the new products. When the final product launches, customers demonstrate strong advocacy because of their involvement and pride in the product.

When customers are psychologically invested in a product, they tend to buy more, spend more, and recommend more, according to Colleen P. Kirk, assistant professor of marketing at New York Institute of Technology.[66]

To build psychological ownership, companies can use at least one of these factors:

- **Enhance control** by allowing customers to have a hand in designing and making the product. Threadless, the T-shirt company, lets users submit original designs and vote on the best ones. Then they print and sell the winners.

- **Encourage "investment of self"** by making products customizable. Research shows that when consumers can personalize products, they buy more and are likely to recommend the products to friends. In Chapter 5,

I explain how some companies allow customers to customize clothes or make their own sneakers. Coca-Cola invited consumers to request customized cans with individual names, and sales rose nearly 3 percent in just 12 weeks.

- **Offer intimate knowledge of the product** to help customers feel like insiders. When customers believe they know every facet of a product or brand, they feel they have a unique relationship with it. Think about a friend who claims to have discovered a band because they knew about it before any of their peers. *Star Wars* fans are notorious for their psychological ownership of a film franchise they know intimately.

How can your company establish psychological ownership by bringing customers into your inner circle?

EXPERIENCE MARKETING

Experience (or *experiential*) *marketing* immerses customers in a brand story through fun, interactive, and mutually beneficial activations.

Every year I attend the massive SXSW conference in Austin, TX. It attracts so many global thought leaders that it has become a festival of experience marketing. Big brands take over every park, restaurant, and street corner in the city to create mind-bending and memorable activations. You might get to experience a virtual reality test drive of a concept Mercedes-Benz, try new gaming technology from Alienware, or meet stars and directors from a blockbuster movie discussing their creative process.

My favorite brand activation was from HBO, promoting their sci-fi series, *Westworld*. Working with the Giant Spoon agency, the network took over a ghost town outside of Austin and transformed it into a set from the television series.

Guests were invited to meet at an Austin bar that HBO had converted into a saloon with iconic props from the set. A bus transported us to the ghost town, where we were greeted by Westworld "hosts" who interacted with us.

In addition to the unbelievable attention to detail in the buildings, characters, and costumes, every guest had a story line. Maybe you had a letter waiting for you at the post office that sent you on a journey through the town. Or you discovered a hidden door, revealing robotic secrets. Perhaps you were caught in the middle of a street fight between the actors and were chased down by the sheriff. There was plenty to eat and drink, all part of the fun.

Nearly every guest captured the amazing activation through video and photography, igniting the experience on social media with a branded hashtag. I hung around for two hours, taking photographs, recording videos, and interviewing some of the characters. Did it work? Well, I put it in my book, didn't I?

Trevor Guthrie of Giant Spoon told me HBO's goal was to create an experience so great that it would "win" SXSW ... and they certainly did, judging by the press coverage and social mentions.

Not every marketing activation has to be that extreme, however. At the same SXSW event, Dell sponsored an evening with famed author Walter Isaacson hosting a panel on robotics. The Case Foundation had a virtual reality display teaching about charities they support. The Brazilian government hosted parties featuring their national music and cuisine in a raucous atmosphere that made you want to visit the country.

What makes for a good branded experience? There are three essential elements, and no shortcuts – you need all of them:

1. Tailor the experience to what you know will delight your customers. Brand experiences must be relevant, and they can only be relevant if you know what makes your customers tick (another reason to get out of the office and visit them!).

2. Don't create experiences that are so far out that consumers don't know what you stand for. Connect the fun to the promise of the brand.

3. Create an experience that is mutually beneficial (often solidified through establishing an emotional connection). Activities that are gratuitous – like exchanging T-shirts for contact info or giving out freebies in a spin-the-wheel game – establish no stickiness, relevance, or value to the relationship. That's a transaction, not an experience. You're attracting people who want a free T-shirt, not a relationship.

In a world where the customer is the marketer, creating a fun and meaningful experience that can get them talking is a timeless strategy for almost any business.

REVIEWS

In the past, brands had control over us because we had to believe what they said – there was no way to test their claims. The internet changed this forever. Reviews, ratings, and comments on almost everything are out there for the world to see. Brands with overly ambitious positioning will be called out. Companies judged to be irresponsible or unethical will face the wrath of the crowd.

Buying is stressful. With all the knowledge of the universe in the palm of our hand, we feel guilty for not making the perfect purchasing decision. Receiving validation before a purchase is much safer, and now, thanks to reviews, it's effortless.

An often-overlooked form of review is the consumer experience video, which is a rising trend.

These folksy, homemade, try-before-you-buy videos may not register on the radar of many companies, but they could be more important than the number of stars you see on common review sites like Yelp and Trip Advisor.

Google's head of ad research and insights, Sara Kleinberg, provided this example:[67] "Before spending on a vacation, people want to understand the real deal. They want to see everything from how other families have fit in the hotel room to the amenities and local attractions ... and even if their kids looked like they were having fun. Luckily for them, people upload review videos of their hotel rooms, of the locations, of things to do."

"Today's consumer is research-obsessed," Sara said. "Doing crazy amounts of research makes people feel more comfortable in their decisions. It provides a sense of security.

"People see videos of other kids having fun at the pool and it becomes real for them. It also shows people what things will be like through the eyes of someone like them – rather than polished website pictures or marketing materials. The 600 percent increase in the time people spend watching review videos on YouTube shows that exploring others' experiences is now a meaningful part of decision making."[68]

For many product categories, user-generated videos provide the most powerful source of reviews, and ultimately sales, including:

- **Automotive:** People film their first day with a new vehicle. There's a whole genre of "first ride" videos sharing how the seats feel, how the radio sounds, and what kind of gas mileage you can expect.
- **Cosmetics:** "First impression" videos are extremely popular, showing people's experience with a makeup product the first time they use it.
- **Food:** People can see firsthand what a fitness enthusiast is eating or what a vegan orders in a restaurant.

While it's perfectly okay to encourage people to leave reviews, never ask a customer to leave you a good review. Just ask your customers to share their experiences. And never offer a discount or a reward for a review, which violates the terms of service of nearly every review site. Besides, nobody trusts a Yelp page filled with nothing but five-star reviews.

In fact, a few negative reviews can actually add credibility. The average Yelp viewer may look at eight to twelve reviews before deciding whether to patronize a business. People are looking for an overall sense of customer satisfaction before they dive in. As long as your reviews are 85 percent positive or greater, you don't need to worry too much about bad reviews.

INFLUENCER MARKETING

In 2012, I published the first book on influencer marketing, *Return On Influence,* and predicted that within two years it would become a mainstream marketing channel. That was one prediction I certainly got right (or at least that's what I tell my mother).

The main idea behind this marketing technique is that brands borrow the trust earned by a person who has worked long and hard to build an engaged audience. Seeing a trusted celebrity, industry thought leader, or even a popular friend post about a brand can create rapid awareness and boost sales. Today, influencer marketing is the hottest and most controversial topic on the marketing scene.

Since I wrote my book, search for the term "influencer marketing" has increased 32,000 percent, and there are now 47 million articles on the topic. So if you want to learn more, there are plenty of resources to guide you! I won't cover anything that you can easily find in a blog post somewhere, but I would like to clear up a few misconceptions.

WHAT IS AN INFLUENCER?

My definition of a *social media influencer* is anyone who posts content that gets shared. It's a person who can move ideas to their own audience and beyond. At a time when trust is under attack, people turn to influencers for authentic advocacy. The more a person can move content to a trusting and relevant audience, the more attractive they are to brands.

When I say "influencer," you might think of YouTube stars selling skateboards, a blogger speaking at a conference, or Kim Kardashian pitching fragrances and makeup tutorials. A lot of the confusion occurs because there are actually five general types of influencers in the world today, all demanding different marketing approaches:

- **Celebrities:** Aligning a brand with a movie star or sports personality began in the early 1900s when Charlie Chaplin and American baseball player Babe Ruth started selling everything from cigarettes to hot dogs. In today's culture, fame breeds trust. Hiring a celebrity is beneficial for a brand needing to quickly establish an image and access a celebrity's fanbase. Celebrities normally have low brand engagement but massive reach. Connecting with these stars can be extremely expensive and risky in an era of social media meltdowns!

- **Macro influencers:** We live in an empowering time when anyone can establish their own influence on the web by publishing content like blogs, videos, podcasts, and visual images. Because of the vast reach of these trusted stars (100,000+ followers), brands are eager to pay for access to their audiences. This may be a legitimate strategy if you need an immediate boost in brand awareness and reputation. However, these content creators are unlikely to commit to a brand without a mutual value exchange (access, information, experiences, or money) and may even turn on a brand if a better deal comes along. Their primary commitment is to their audience, not necessarily a product or idea.

- **Professional:** This group might have 20,000 to 100,000 followers and includes journalists, business leaders, authors, and subject matter experts. You'll find them speaking at conferences because they have high authority. They love engaging with a brand if it means access to executives and information that enhances their status and expertise.

- **Micro influencers:** This group is getting a lot of attention from brands because they have a large, trusting audience (1,000 to 20,000 followers) and can't get enough of your brand. They're relevant to brand conversations and proud to be associated with you. They occasionally might require compensation for their expenses, but they simply love getting your products and gear to show off to their friends.

- **Brand advocates:** These everyday folks are also sometimes called *nano influencers* because they have fewer than 1,000 followers. They don't think of themselves as influencers. They just love to share content about their daily lives and make you part of it if they're fans. They have a small network but may be your best and most passionate customers. A lot of brand attention has been going to this category because it's relatively inexpensive, effective, and drama-free.

So, not all influencer marketing is the same. There's a broad spectrum of individuals a brand can connect with and many different strategies and outcomes.

Technically, there is a sixth category of influencers: Pets. Instagram favorites like Jiffpom the adorable Pomeranian (@jiffpom) with 7 million followers and Grumpy Cat (@RealGrumpyCat) with 2.4 million followers make big bank for their owners. I've attempted to enter this category with my pet goldfish Sushi (@TheRealSushi) but I can't get him (her?) to sit still for the Instagram shot. He has such a short attention span.

(Return to serious)

INFLUENCERS BECOME TRUSTED FRIENDS

Despite the very real benefits brands can realize from influencer marketing, there's still a lot of skepticism, especially when follower counts and engagement can be faked. Several high-profile scandals have rocked the confidence that some brands have in this tactic. It seems that when any social media strategy gets popular, it soon becomes corrupted.

But with diligence and persistence, there's no denying influencer marketing works – nearly 50 percent of 25-to-34-year-olds say they have been motivated to try a new product solely on the recommendation of a social media influencer.[69] It's not unusual for fashion, cosmetics, and entertainment brands to attribute huge sales gains to recommendations from influencers.

Influencers are seen as warm, competent, and most important, effective. On average, they have between 400 percent and 700 percent higher rate of consumer engagement over a company's branded posts. Influencers operate at the grassroots level of social media, offering personalized responses and attention to the unique needs and requests of each follower, which is impossible for big companies to scale.[70]

Influencer marketing is an indispensable strategy for industries such as fashion, food, entertainment, music, consumer electronics, gaming, and travel. But it's not just a consumer product strategy. Brands like Microsoft, SAP, Samsung, and Oracle have sophisticated programs that place their business influencers in the same respected category as analysts and members of the press.

"Our intention is to never have an influencer sell our products," said Konstanze Alex, who oversees influencer relations for Dell Technologies. "And that is supported all the way through our culture. Yes of course there is a temptation to want an influencer to say, 'buy this or that,' but our team is very clear from the beginning that we will never expect that in the relationship.

"Our goal is to use these experts to raise the awareness of what we can do, the capabilities we have, but not at all to sell. We've created a training workshop for marketers where we clearly outline what's involved in influencer relations, which it should actually be called, instead of marketing. These relationships are very important, they're long-term, and they're trust-based."[71]

An influencer strategy is also relevant for small companies. My friend John Phillips is the founder of Phillips Forged, a most unusual business. John reclaims steel from old structures, plows, and sawmill blades to make heirloom-quality, handcrafted knives.

John was a fan of Sean Brock, a James Beard Award-winning chef who resides in Nashville, and had been trying to make a connection with him over social media.

With a little luck, John got to meet Sean at a Nashville craft fair. When the chef heard the story behind the handcrafted knives, he wanted to make it part of the heritage of his own Husk restaurants and bought steak knives John had at his booth.

The famous chef proudly posted a photo of his new find on Instagram. This authentic advocacy from a respected thought leader was better than any advertisement John could have paid for. It accessed an entirely new audience who loved this chef and the craft of cooking.

"In a day, my email box was full of inquiries for new orders," John said. "That photo had an immediate impact on my business." Within a week, John had added thousands of followers on Instagram and acquired $40,000 in new orders. And all those new customers will have Phillips Forged stories to tell.

INFLUENCER MARKETING VS. WOMM

There's obvious overlap between word-of-mouth marketing and influencer marketing, but there are three main differences:

In WOMM, a story is "set free" through conversations with the hope that if it's authentic, relevant, and interesting, people will repeatedly share it. With influencers, you know the story will move because the individual has a dependable track record. This also makes some influencer measurement easier because established personalities normally have readily available metrics.

In WOMM, super sharers naturally pick up your story and organically spread it. With an influencer, the arrangement usually requires some value exchange – an experience, exclusive information, access to products, or even a paycheck.

Influencer marketing has more regulatory burdens than WOMM in most countries. If an influencer is paid to promote a product, it must be disclosed as an advertisement.

Will influencer marketing last? Yes, for a simple reason: Influencers are more than influencers. They are perceived as experts and friends. And friends trust friends on the island.

SOCIAL PROOF, SOCIAL VALIDATION, AND CALLS TO ACTION

Studies show that digital natives might check the web four or five times during the consideration phase before completing even a small-value purchase. What will they find?

In this world of overwhelming choice, people are desperate for clues about the best people to follow, the right leaders to believe, and the ideal products to buy – especially expensive products.

That's why building robust *social proof* is essential to reinforcing the consideration process. Social proof helps customers confirm they're making the right choice. Social proof might include:

- Testimonies
- Reviews
- Photos and videos of you and your happy customers
- Awards
- Social media presence

Social validation means providing backup to the story consumers might be hearing through user-generated content, word-of-mouth marketing, and reviews. Remember my story of the Room & Board furniture company from Chapter 3? When I heard about the company, it had entered into the consideration phase, and when I checked their website, these stories were validated by content from their customers and suppliers.

Finally, you'll need an innovative approach for translating traffic beyond simple awareness to real brand consideration. Providing some sort of *call to action* can keep people interested and engaged with your brand.

For example, when you visit L'Oreal's website, you can learn new ways to apply makeup. On the Charles Schwab investment site, you can find a tool to learn the basics of financial planning. Gilt Groupe, the online luxury goods site, teaches you about the company's unique business model and how to get access to great deals. Dell provides a free tool to help you assess your company's progress with digital transformation.

The goal in each case is to highlight a unique offer that persuades consumers to learn more about the brand and helps the company earn purchase consideration.

THE TRUTH ABOUT SOCIAL MEDIA

Unfortunately, we're in a long season of disillusionment with social media. Beyond its well-documented problems with hate speech, election malfeasance, and emotional manipulation, large blocks of consumers are running away from a social web that has lost its joy and innocence.

And yet, social media plays an extraordinary role in the conversation engine ... but perhaps it's a different role than you expect.

A popular term in our field is *social media marketing.* If you think about it, combining those words is a death knell for brands. Social media is a place where our customers form their like-minded islands to connect to friends, see pictures of the new baby, celebrate milestones, watch funny videos, and share breaking news. It's not a place where people want to be marketed to. In fact, they avoid that.

The first book to forecast how businesses *should* show up on social media was *The Cluetrain Manifesto.* The authors envisioned a dynamic in which consumer conversations would rule the business world *(they have)* and companies would organically join in with a human voice *(they have not).*

But social media became too popular, too fast. It didn't take long for businesses to require the ROI of every tweet, post, and photo as the framework for strategy. Instead of recognizing social media as an opportunity to strengthen the customer connection, companies did what they always do: blanket people with ads, drive cheap "impressions," and squeeze revenue from every post and tweet. Sadly, businesses erased the "social" from "social media."

- Conversations gave way to broadcasting "content."
- Social media became an IT function and automated to the point of being soulless.
- Humans with personalities and names were replaced by corporate personas and branded voices.
- Success was measured in clicks and likes rather than relationships and loyalty.
- Social media's primary role evolved to become a place to weaponize influencers.

Rather than fundamentally changing how marketing works, marketing fundamentally changed how social media works. Social media now accounts for more than one in eight dollars spent on marketing, and it's forecast to keep growing.[72]

So, how do we consider our social media strategy in the context of the Third Rebellion?

Let's go back to the islander analogy and a human-centered approach to marketing. Social media can be an effective way to serve the islanders if it can:

- Provide relevant human connections.
- Form reliable and trustworthy communication channels.
- Express shared values.

- Display human emotions like compassion, understanding, and empathy.
- Create unique and entertaining experiences.
- Demonstrate active involvement in local issues.
- Offer a dependable way to respond in a moment of customer need.

Those digital islands are probably represented somewhere in the social media landscape – Facebook Groups, Reddit forums, LinkedIn Groups, Snapchat friends, Twitter Lists, and other popular online assemblies.

I've railed against the misuse of digital advertising, but skillful promotion through social media can be an effective method to support all these goals. The ability to hyper-target can help you discover relevant islands, connect to the islanders who need you most, and let them know how you might belong.

Finally, social media is an excellent way to quietly listen and learn. What's going on in those island communities? How are things changing, and what meaningful role can we play in that group?

In summary, social media still provides an essential chance to connect to customers and serve them, but most companies are missing the opportunity due to an outdated focus on "me-centric posts," random acts of content, and misguided attempts to manufacture engagement.

CONTENT MARKETING

Closely related to social media marketing is *content marketing*. Content is the fuel for social media. Social media is a distribution channel for content.

To give you an idea of the relative importance of "branded" content, I'd like you to participate in a painless experiment. Think about how many corporate content channels you subscribe to and view at least once a month. This includes things like a company blog, newsletter, podcast, or YouTube channel.

I've asked this question hundreds of times in classes and workshops, and the highest number ever reported was five. Most people answer, "two or less."

If you're reading this book, you're probably a marketing professional or you want to be one. So, you're into this stuff. And yet, you don't subscribe to much business content. Which means almost nobody subscribes to business content!

The research supports this, of course, and tells us that marketers can rarely detect if their content is working (several studies show that 80 percent of content on a B2B website is never seen). Given these facts, it seems weird that producing even more content is the fastest-growing line item on most marketing budgets these days.

The *inbound marketing* concept purports that relevant and excellent content auto-magically attracts eyeballs to our website in a highly efficient manner. But even Dharmesh Shah, a HubSpot founder and pioneer of this idea, admitted that content marketing is mostly pay-to-play today. It normally only works with a boost from paid ads.[73] That brings us right back to the beginning of the book – who wants to enact a strategy that requires paying for more ads that nobody sees or believes?

If the content marketing world is such a noisy mess, why are so many companies producing prodigious amounts of new content? Because they're afraid not to. Everybody else is doing it, and it seems risky to not follow the herd. This is an industry built on the hyperbolic hope of extreme case studies. We see a few companies experiencing wild success with content marketing and naturally extrapolate that it must be good for everyone, every time.

I'm not the anti-content dude. It's absolutely essential to many marketing efforts, including my own and that of many of my clients. But like social media, it's time to reconsider the hype of content marketing in a rational new perspective.

1. Content should be viewed with the same esteem as your company's products. It's not just sales propaganda. It should be good enough to be a stand-alone product that customers look forward to receiving. If you can't meet that standard of quality, you'll certainly fail in this era of overwhelming information density.

2. A content plan is more or less your search engine optimization plan. SEO is still important for some businesses ... but not as many as you might think.

Unless you have the resources to land among the top three search terms in your market area, it's a fruitless effort that will be further imperiled by the increasing use of voice search. However, if you're SEO-inclined, a content plan is essential.

3. The primary value of content for most businesses is either to establish authority or to entertain. Both strategies are effective to attract and retain customers if you're committed to creating superior content consistently over time.

4. *Earned media,* or the sharing of content, is a widely used marketing term that's misunderstood. I regard social sharing as one of the best digital marketing metrics because it's a sign of *advocacy.* The economic value of content that is not seen and shared is zero. This means a strategy for igniting your content through an audience is more important than the strategy to create the content in the first place. (Consult my book *The Content Code* for a framework on how to do this.)

5. For many businesses today, the product itself is a story – people are buying a narrative more than a physical good. Content can be important to establishing and sustaining that narrative, as we witnessed with Room & Board and YETI.

6. Content distributed through social media can serve as a reminder to have a conversation about a product.

7. Increasingly, content acts as the B2B salesforce. Busy purchasing executives are calling on a human sales rep later and later in the purchasing cycle. "Today more than ever, we build customer relationships not face-to-face but through content," said Andrea L. Ames, CEO of Idyllic Point. "When you realize that content has a bigger relationship-building potential than talking to a salesperson, that's huge. Your content is your sales opportunity. The people who read your content aren't researching just for themselves. They curate it. They share it with executives, who send it out to their evaluation teams. Your readers are influencers."[74]

Some sort of content is the epicenter of most customer conversations, but it's time to adjust our strategy from "cover the world with content" to one precisely tuned to create conversations, consideration, and most important, social sharing.

"NEW" CYCLES

There's a lot of overlap in the marketing tactics I've named so far. Word-of-mouth marketing can lead to user-generated content. Reviews can be used as social proof and so on.

But all these ideas need fuel. There has to be something to talk about, and in this era of constant consideration, brands need to consistently generate something that is newsworthy.

Interesting news is a powerful trigger for sharing. People who share content the most are news junkies. They want to show they're on top of the latest products, news, trends, and ideas.

Marketing industry leader Mitch Joel contends that innovation is critical to creating conversations today. "Brands have made businesses lazy," he said. "All the energy is being spent in the battle of perceptions instead of true product innovations. A lack of product innovation is to blame for much of the loss of customer loyalty. If you want to create conversations, create something worthy of a discussion."

Marketing must think of itself in terms of serving a news cycle through meaningful product innovations and conversational events and announcements.

SUPPORTING THE 13 PERCENT

Across most industries, just 13 percent of your customers can be considered loyal. How do you help these special people spread your story?

In this chapter, I've provided many practical ideas to influence the two-thirds of the marketing that is taking place without you. Your most loyal customers are the ones most likely to do it for you. You're already on their island!

Whether you choose to focus on word-of-mouth marketing, creating meaningful experiences, or building peak moments, your most loyal customers are power lines transmitting your content and creating new business value. Boston Consulting Group showed that these advocates are responsible for 800 percent more revenue than your shop-around customers.

For many years, I've asked the participants of my university classes – all seasoned marketing professionals – if they know, by name, who is sharing their content the most. Even for the largest companies, we're not talking about millions of people here. Maybe a couple hundred at most, and for many companies it's a few dozen or less. I call this special group the *Alpha Audience.* They're the transmitters driving the most marketing value to your organization. And every time I ask, my question is received by blank stares.

Shouldn't we be celebrating these loyalists and treating them in extraordinary ways?

I'm not referring to mechanized and math-driven loyalty programs. I'm talking about creating surprising experiences for the ones who are out there singing your praises. Those people are your marketing department!

I think the Alpha Audience strategy is very simple ... just two steps.

First, you have to create and sustain a system to methodically find these people. That means going beyond the charts and graphs of your social media dashboard. It might require sampling individual social media posts about your company or reading all of them if you're a small business. It could mean conditioning your customer service department to be aware when they've discovered a true fan or rewarding account managers for nurturing that rare loyalty as well as achieving their sales goals.

Step two can be summed up in two words: *unexpected delight.*

Even the surliest curmudgeon is going to talk about your company in glowing terms if you thrill him in a surprising way. Companies like Ralph Lauren, Adidas, and Target have even created secret smartphone apps to constantly delight their best customers.

The best sources of unexpected delight won't necessarily come from a strategy or a script. Getting a free bottle of water in a hotel room isn't unexpected delight. Getting an elephant in your room is another story. And here it is:

My friend Andrew Grill was staying at the Waldorf Astoria Ras al Khaimah in the UAE when he received a text message from the staff. The exchange went like this:

> *Kateryna: How is your stay going so far? Please let us know if we may assist you for the remainder of your stay. Thank you!*
>
> *Andrew: I need an elephant in my room this evening please.*
>
> *Kateryna: Absolutely Mr. Grill. It would be my pleasure to arrange an elephant for your room this evening. Any particular time you would like her delivered?*
>
> *Andrew: I was joking!*
>
> *Kateryna: You ask, we deliver!*

That evening, a toy elephant was waiting in his room, as well as an elephant made from bath towels. Of course Andrew transmitted his delight throughout his social channels. And now we have his moment of delight recorded forever in a book.

Surprising and delighting your customers doesn't have to be extravagant. But you do need to nurture an employee culture empowered to express empathy at the right moment.

If the service representative dealing with these crucial customers is the least-experienced and lowest-paid person in your company, you're jeopardizing your most important marketing opportunity. Don't just pay people to be a customer service placeholder. Pay them to ignite conversations with unexpected delight.

REBALANCING ACT

This chapter has documented just a few ways we can reimagine marketing in a human-centered way.

I hope you have lot of new ideas. But an idea is just the beginning. You must be able to act on it, and that means rebalancing your budget, your priorities, your organization, and even your agency relationships.

In the next section of the book, I introduce you to some inspiring marketers who are finding creative new ways to get an invitation to the customer islands. Finally, I'll explore the organizational implications of this new marketing mindset.

PART FOUR

MARKETING REIMAGINED

CHAPTER 10

THE PATHFINDERS

"Great companies have something in common:
They don't try to matter by winning.
They win by mattering."
—BERNADETTE JIWA

It will take years of effort, dramatic cultural change, and perhaps a few retirements before some companies can adopt a human-centered marketing approach.

In this chapter, I provide inspiration and encouragement through the stories of innovative marketing leaders already carving bright new paths.

THE MARKETING OF NO MARKETING

Last year, my son announced he was getting married, and in a moment of paternal insanity, I agreed to host the wedding and reception at my home.

I wanted to make every detail perfect, and of course that started with the choice of beer (right?). I offered to order some kegs from a favorite local microbrewery, but my son said he would handle it. To my amazement, on the day of the wedding his friends rolled up with coolers filled to the brim with cans of Pabst Blue Ribbon, better known as PBR.

I used to work in the beverage industry, and PBR was considered a bottom-of-the-barrel brand. It didn't have celebrity spokesmodels, TV ads, or its own brewery – it leased capacity from other companies back then. There was even a rumor that PBR consisted of any leftover beer the contract brewers could use to fill the cans.

And yet, undeniably, PBR has become the drink of choice for a young American generation. I always wondered ... how was this possible? And then I met Ted Wright.

Ted may be the most unlikely marketing genius I've ever known. He was captain of his high school math team and studied mathematics under Stephen Hawking at Cambridge University. But he was fascinated by business, too, and when he pursued an MBA at the University of Chicago, he saw the light. Literally.

"Back then, the students in the computer lab were just starting to use search engines," he said. "The two leading services at the time were Alta Vista and Yahoo. The room always glowed red and blue from the screens of these services. Then one day I walked in, and the room glowed white. Everybody had switched to Google – without any advertising or promotion. How did that happen so fast? How does a product go viral?"

He began studying everything he could about how new products spread and discovered a largely ignored field of word-of-mouth marketing. It was all about math, really, and the math made sense to Ted.

- 70 percent of word-of-mouth conversations happen face-to-face.

- 15 percent of those conversations mention a branded product or service.

- 20 percent of all brands in the U.S. are sold through recommendations from friends.

This means that an average person is having 112 marketing conversations a week, and they're talking about 56 different brands. And about 10 percent of the population (those super-sharers from Chapter 9) has 50 percent more conversations and talks about 100 percent more brands!

It dawned on Ted that this is how the search screens turned white, and in fact, this is how much of business must get done in America. Not through glossy ads or PR spin, but through people. And America was largely ignoring it. This was a business opportunity.

He started his own small agency (called Fizz) and began to experiment with his formula-based marketing ideas. If you trust the numbers, it would undoubtedly work. And Ted is a guy who trusts the numbers.

Then PBR called.

While people like me saw a brand that had been sinking since the 1970s, Ted considered PBR a fascinating story, and stories spread when they're in the right hands.

He began to hang around bars in Portland and Pittsburgh, talking to people about what they were drinking and why. A generation of millennials were coming of age and striving to find their independent voice. And they detested marketing.

What happens if a brand identity isn't created through ads and the company owners ... but by consumers?

"The worst transgression for this generation was to do something just because you wanted to be seen doing it, whether it was drinking a particular brand of beer or driving a certain kind of car," Ted said. "The key word was 'authentic.' So they swarmed to things that the mainstream culture deemed hopelessly unhip. At the time, nothing was less hip than PBR.

"The fact that PBR had no money for traditional advertising was a blessing in disguise. Throwing a bunch of TV commercials on the air would have been a disaster. The fact that these young people had never seen a PBR ad was a huge selling point for them. Traditional advertising, particularly the kind produced by big beer companies, would have killed the brand. In fact, any indication that the brand was trying too hard to be liked would have backfired. Our human-based approach is exactly what this brand needed.

"The trick was to get the most influential people among this already influential group of early hipsters to talk to their friends about PBR. All we had to do was give them good stories to share.

"We discovered that people loved PBR for being unpretentious and low profile. So we hit the streets and started offering our support to creative people doing cool, interesting things just for the sake of it.

"If we found young people having bike messenger races, we were there. We brought beer and hats to gallery openings, skating parties, juggling contests – you name it. We gave six packs of beer to Mini Kiss, a Kiss tribute band whose members were all little people. And we never just handed out stuff and walked away. We talked to these young people about the stuff they were into. And of course, we talked about the beer."

Slowly but surely, the brand grew. In year one of the marketing effort, PBR grew 5 percent. In years two and three, it grew 15 percent. By year four, PBR was featured in a *New York Times Magazine* story with the headline, "The Marketing of No Marketing."

By year five, PBR could be found in the coolest bars in the country and had recorded a combined annual growth of 55 percent. The brand had grown a minimum of 10 percent in every American state and 50 percent in more than 30 states. Despite the success, the brand resisted spending on redesigns and splashy new ads because that would look like marketing.

Today, Ted's Fizz Agency is an established success, and the Atlanta home office is buzzing with interesting people dreaming up "talkable" stories for dozens of brands. On a wall, he has an original piece of art made for the office that declares "TV is dead."

"I can't go out and really say that," he said, "because there are thousands of them and one of me.

"But it is."

MAKE THE LOGO BIGGER? MAYBE NOT

One of the aspects of the localism movement I mention in Chapter 5 is an outright rejection of big branding and logos. There's even a cottage industry emerging in New York City that carefully removes logos from clothes!

The book *No Logo* by journalist Naomi Klein is about the rapacious incursion of brands and marketing into every sphere of public life. She documents the grassroots backlash against this trend, especially among young people. Klein said this repercussion is feeding the consumer rebellion against marketing and fueling a dissent-based lifestyle. At some point, we would expect people would rise up and say, "Enough is enough."

One sign of the anti-brand movement is marketing that has so little branding, so little selling, that it may be difficult to tell who is behind it at all. You may be wondering if I've lost my mind, but nonbranded branding is quite a fascinating and legitimate idea.

My favorite example of this concept can be experienced in a small YouTube film called "First Kiss" by Tatia Pilieva. The short, black-and-white film documents what happens when 20 strangers meet for the first time and are asked to kiss each other on camera. It's touching, thought-provoking, and provocative. Let's use this example to run a little multimedia experiment. If you're near an online device, please view this video on YouTube right now.

If you watched the video, could you tell who sponsored it? I've shown this film to hundreds of students in my college classes and not one of them could answer the question. And yet, in the first moments of the film, the words "Wren presents" appear. The introduction is so ephemeral and subtle that this content can correctly be characterized as unbranded!

What's behind this story?

Boutique online clothing retailer Wren faced the ultimate marketing dilemma: how to create a conversational moment for a start-up (in the crowded fashion market!) on a low budget.

Wren's founder, Melissa Coker, was up to the challenge. Melissa spent her early career in New York working in the magazine industry for titles like *Vogue* and *W* before relocating to Los Angeles. One day, a void in her wardrobe led Melissa to design a few pieces of her own, which ended up being the start of her own fashion label, and in 2007, Wren was born.

In a crowded market like fashion, just doing what everybody else is doing could never work, so Melissa came up with the idea of getting her friends together and asking them to kiss ... while the camera rolled.

The film cost just $1,500 to make. The content felt ... artisanal. It was handcrafted, gritty, real, and risky.

But it has been viewed more than 150 million times on YouTube. "First Kiss" received significant mainstream media coverage, including *The New York Times, CNN, The Guardian,* and *Harper's Bazaar,* propelling Wren into the national spotlight.

The genius of Melissa's film is that it created a massive emotional response to the universal awkwardness and beauty of a first kiss. It wasn't about clothing, although it did feature Wren fashions on the kissers. If you were the one in a million who saw the name briefly at the beginning, you still wouldn't know it was a clothing company. But the film created such a frenzy (both positive and negative) that people dug deep to find out who was behind it. Here are the results, directly attributed to the unbranded film:

- 1,400 percent increase in sales
- 15,000 percent increase in traffic
- 96 percent were first-time visitors

Unbranded content isn't for everyone, but it's certainly a way to stand out and create conversations in a noisy world. It has been used as a technique in pharmaceuticals, consumer packaged goods, and retail. If you're going to try it, the content needs to:

- Take a risk.
- Be conversation-worthy in a way that sparks curiosity.
- Tap into a strong emotion.

- Build momentum. The "First Kiss" video was not a one-off. Wren created a series of small films to keep the conversations going.

"We make these fashion films every season now," Melissa said in an interview.[75] "I strive to make an interesting film that exists on its own rather than something that feels like a commercial, and it seems to be touching people – not only people who are in fashion, but also random people who haven't connected to us at all."

VALUES FIRST

In Chapter 7, I explored how huge companies like Nike and American Eagle are conforming to customer values to ignite loyalty. I thought it would be interesting to share the story of a small business in the Netherlands that is built entirely on a single ideal.

Nearly 20 years ago, Dutch journalist Teun (Tony) van de Keuken was shocked when he read a book about child slavery on cocoa farms in West Africa. Slavery still existed? He decided to find out for himself and created an investigative television program to expose the truth.

It turns out that child slavery is alarmingly common in West Africa, the source of 70 percent of the world's cocoa. According to a Tulane University study, the current estimate is that 2.3 million children are working in illegal circumstances, trafficking, and forced labor in West Africa alone. Sometimes the children have to use large machetes and lift heavy loads, and they're exposed to pesticides. Because they're being forced to do heavy manual labor during the day, many children are unable to go to school.

The circumstances are even more appalling when you consider that large chocolate makers signed an international agreement pledging to ban child labor in 2001.

While he was working on his investigative report, Tony contacted every major chocolate manufacturer in the world, but nobody would talk to him. When the show aired, he ate a pile of chocolate bars and turned himself in to the Dutch authorities as a chocolate criminal, claiming that he was supporting a system of slavery.

Horrified by what he found, he decided to take dramatic action and created his own chocolate company – Tony's Chocolonely – devoted to eradicating child slavery in the cocoa industry. Tony set about creating transparent, fair, long-term relationships with ethical cocoa farmers from whom his company sources directly.

At six partner cooperatives in Ghana and Côte d'Ivoire, Tony's Chocolonely works with 5,500 independent farmers to improve their yields using sustainable farming practices. It provides farmers with agricultural education while paying them a living wage so they can hire adult workers and send their kids to school.

By eradicating the anonymity that is often conveniently baked into the supply chain, Tony's Chocolonely takes full responsibility for the entire system. It pays farmers 20 percent more to secure the slave-free supply chain.

Tony's company doesn't invest in any traditional marketing and instead uses its product to speak directly to the consumer and spur word-of-mouth conversations and referrals.

For example, the chocolate bars, available in 19 flavors, are split into uneven chunks instead of conventional even-sized pieces. This draws attention to the "unevenness" and unethical practices in the industry. The inside of the wrapper has a story about the company's mission with ideas of what everybody can do to stamp out slavery.

Although the company has a serious side, the joy of chocolate is reflected in the bright packaging and playful designs used to tell its story. Every package and customer interaction is viewed as an opportunity to spread a story about the values and mission of the company.

Tony's Chocolonely is also committed to business transparency and shares its detailed business plan and roadmap on its website. It points out both its successes and failures. It's a great case study in values-based marketing in a way that helps the customers tell the company's story ... and it's working. The business is profitable and expanding rapidly. Its products can be found in a growing number of online and physical retailers.

Most important, Tony's competitors are beginning to notice. Now that Tony's Chocolonely is making a dent in the $100 billion chocolate business, the biggest manufacturers are being forced to reflect on the problems in their own supply chains and find solutions.

Once you know Tony's story, it's hard to look at chocolate the same way ever again. I'm making their products regular gifts for my family and friends to help spread his story. Like many of Tony's loyal fans, I have become his marketing department.

THE MARKETING ANTHROPOLOGIST

What is branding today?

We'd like to think it's about us and our magical marketing machine. Color, shape, data, vision, tension, design, personas, identity, beauty, simplicity. But the greatest brands resonate and spread like wildfire because they tap into an ability to see and understand the minute details of life that others don't see.

And that's what Martin Lindstrom does. I regard Martin as one of the greatest marketers on Earth, but his gift is simple: He notices the details and connects those intimate customer truths to brands.

Martin is an anthropologist. He plops himself into people's homes, workplaces, and shopping experiences to discover the nooks and crannies of the human experience that translate into massive business insights.

It all started with his set of Legos.

When Martin was 12 years old, he was employed by Lego's R&D department. Lego wanted to learn from its customers, and the customers were kids, so they signed up Martin to play with Legos. The experience made an indelible impact on his future career.

"As I grew older, I started to look at myself from two points of view," he said. "Yes, I'm a kid, I'm playing, I have fun. But I also started observing myself the way Lego would observe me. Metaphorically, it was as if I had a camera on myself and I was noticing *how* I was playing and *why* I was playing. I became curious about the behavior of playing. When I was together with my friends, I would ask them questions to see if they played like I did. I began to think like a Lego marketer."

As Martin entered the business world, he noticed a disconnect. Marketers were focused on internal politics and irrelevant metrics instead of meaningful innovations that served their customers.

"The immune system for change in the organization is just too high," he said. "Even though a business sees it needs to change, it's just too hard, too much of a fight. So nothing gets done. Consumers are *driving* business right now, and their voices are much stronger than they have ever been. We need, as companies and brands, to listen to them, but the organizations are not geared for that. They're too busy pleasing themselves and their bureaucracy. They look inside, not outside. They've lost any concept of reality.

"I'm on a mission to get the companies closer to consumers because there is no way around it right now. The game is already running, and it is being run by the consumer. How do we adjust? By destroying all bureaucracy, politics, and those internal KPIs which are completely detached from reality. We need to focus on one factor driving the organizations and that is the customer. I do that by bringing the customers to the businesses and the businesses to the customers, so they meet every day."

When I spoke with Martin, he was on his way to a client in Miami. "I have one of the largest companies in the world joining me tomorrow, and we're going to visit ordinary homes here in Miami neighborhoods," he said. "They take off the tie, they dress down, the consumers have no idea where we come from, and we go out and see reality. These executives have never done that before in their lives. Sad but true."

Martin has transformed his customers by connecting them to constant human truths. He has worked with dozens of leading brands, but he mentioned a case study from Swiss International Airlines as a favorite example of his work.

"Swiss Air is one of the larger airlines in Europe, and they asked us to redesign the economy class. If you do insight with the passengers, they'll tell you they want to change the leg room, the food service, and the price. No surprises. If that was the only conclusion of my research, I should be fired on the spot, because that would be the wrong question to ask.

"A better question is, 'How do you *feel* when you're flying economy class?' And the answer we learned – by actually getting onboard and working with passengers – was this: 'anxiety.' Anxiety of being late to the airport, anxiety about security, anxiety about storing your little carry-on, anxiety about baggage you may never see again, anxiety getting up to immigration and you're last in line.

"In the old days of marketing, we would probably never address anxiety because we would be bragging about all our new planes or something, but let's say we did. We would have addressed this by doing an ad campaign thinking this would somehow calm anxiety, and we would distribute some vouchers we believed would magically calm our nervous customers.

"What we did was very different. First, we opened up a communication channel between the people working on the ground and the employees in the sky. So, when a Swiss Air plane is descending into New York, the captain will announce, 'Ladies and gentlemen, we'll land at JFK in 40 minutes. I hope you had a pleasant flight, and I have some great news for you. We will arrive at gate 109. It doesn't seem like great news, but it is because it's only a six-minute walk from immigration. Even better, I spoke to the head of immigration who tells me that the waiting time is only 17 minutes, and the waiting time for the baggage is only 18 minutes. So, with a bit of luck, you'll be through the airport in half an hour. I've also been in touch with our ground representatives who tell me it's averaging a 27-minute drive to Manhattan by the time you get your baggage. So, if this is your home, you'll arrive in less than 90 minutes from now.'

"That is a message that is removing anxiety. This is very different from conventional marketing, but it is the essence of what we do, because it still comes back to customer satisfaction and earning their trust.

"CMOs can no longer just be shepherds of the marketing dashboard. They must be infusing our customer needs into every part of the organization and facilitating responses around this one purpose, our customer. That purpose, that drive, must be made clear to everyone in the company. That is the CMO we need today."

TRANSPARENT CLOTHING

I was hosting young friends at my home when one young woman excitedly started talking about her obsession with Everlane, an online clothing retailer. I became curious. This was just the type of person who was supposed to be *rejecting* mainstream retail brands.

"What makes them so different?" I asked her.

"Well, they just put $40 in my account as a thank you," she said. "No strings attached. But of course I immediately spent the money on more Everlane clothes ... and the number of people I've told about it? Well, I've sold at least $600 worth of stuff for them this week."

The customer is the marketer. Everlane is a company that understands that.

The company was started by Michael Preysman, who, in 2011, was a 25-year-old computer science major working at an investment firm. He dreamed of starting his own enterprise, one that made *stuff* rather than software, and he saw an opportunity to disrupt retail. Clothes are cheap to make, but they're marked-up dramatically after they leave the factory floor – wholesalers, retailers, and various middlemen all take a cut.

In a little more than five years, Michael had built a $250 million company with almost no advertising. That's unheard of in the fashion industry.

At first glance, Everlane seems ordinary. Maybe even dull. It offers neat, minimalist designs at a reasonable price. But from a marketing perspective, the company is on the leading edge.

The marketing formula for most retail brands is pretty standard: price, performance, and lifestyle. The trick is to explain the difference about your price, performance, and lifestyle through ads, packaging, store displays, and contracts with high-priced models. That's expensive. And for a new company, it's impossible.

The beauty of Everlane is that it describes its value in a way that can be told through stories, the actions of the company, the design of their site, and most important, their fans. It's radical transparency.

By selling direct and online, Everlane can be profitable by charging about twice what the product costs to make. By contrast, full retail typically charges eight to ten times the price of production. For any piece of clothing on the Everlane site, you can see a simple diagram explaining how much it cost to make and the company's profit margin.

Everlane's business model is designed around simplicity:

- Minimal designs with minimum inventory
- Almost no sales or promotions
- No middlemen

But fashion industry insiders claim the company's true genius is its marketing team. The Everlane group is constantly looking for online and offline human touchpoints. Here are a few examples:

- Product launches are accompanied by beautiful photo stories evoking the "effortlessly chic" aesthetic. Photos often feature the designers or the brand's long-time customers (of every shape and size), fostering a sense of authentic connection with the brand.

- Instagram campaigns like #whereItravel encourage fans to show off their Everlane products and summer vacation photos. That campaign ended with more than 11,000 user-generated submissions – a significant level of storytelling for a relatively small fan base.

- In line with its minimalist, anti-consumerism commitment, on Black Friday (the major holiday shopping day in America), Everlane donates all profits to workers at its factories.

By focusing on consumer-driven marketing, Everlane disrupted the traditional retail system and is the most human company in its space.

LEANING INTO CUSTOMER MOMENTS

In the early days of television, programming hours were filled by local talent – cooking shows, variety shows, and craft shows. Not many people were watching back then, so TV's pioneers had to be creative to fill the airwaves.

It was easy to advertise back then, too. In my hometown of Knoxville, TN, most of the TV advertising in those early days was dominated by a local grocer named Cas Walker. In between programs, he would talk about his grocery store and repeat his business tagline, "Nobody Can Beat My Meat." That tagline wouldn't work so well today, but in an emerging marketing channel, it only took a little homespun content to earn an audience.

Today, it takes a lot more than a local cooking show to capture your customer's attention. It takes *Game of Thrones*. People have so many choices that they want to experience something unique and epic.

Marc Simons, co-founder of the Giant Spoon agency, is in the business of unique and epic.

As a child, Marc discovered he had a natural marketing talent while helping out at his family's pet food store in upstate New York. In college, he was an early adopter of social media and had new digital insights that were in high demand as companies tried to unlock the secrets of Facebook and YouTube.

Eventually this led to career opportunities with agencies in Los Angeles, where he found innovative ways to combine emerging technologies with traditional marketing.

"My job was to stay on the edge of new," he said, "to find the next big thing and be an early adopter for clients like Home Depot and CBS. I was the one pitching wacky ideas. In fact, the wackiest of wacky ideas. But these were companies that had the budget to try some things in emerging media. For example, we put the first video screen in a magazine for CBS. So, you open up the magazine and the video screen started playing.

"I learned that the secret sauce to marketing in a noisy world was coming up with something so innovative, so crazy, so conversational, that it would earn massive attention from the media and our customers. My job became creating ideas that people want to talk about. Create something people are going to want to share. Create something *they would pay for.* I wanted to make something that had never been made before."

Eventually, that became the core competency of his own marketing agency, Giant Spoon. "We didn't just want to make the pre-roll ahead of the thing that people actually want to see," he said. "We wanted to *be the thing* that people want to see. If we can pull that off, then that's the perfect place to be today."

An example of this experiential marketing is an activation the company designed and built to promote the movie *Blade Runner 2049* at the annual Comic-Con International event.

"I started to think ... what would a fully immersive Blade Runner theme park ride look like that would pop up for four days at Comic-Con? Could we dream that up?

"Warner Brothers and Alcon Entertainment showed us key art for the film, and we were really attracted to this one bar scene. What if people could go into that bar? What does that look like? What does that gloomy and damp Los Angeles in 2049 feel like? We thought that could be a very cool experience."

The Giant Spoon team took over a site near the San Diego Convention Center and built a huge black circus tent for the activation. They created a 4D theater with seats that moved and virtual reality headsets that took you on a wild, futuristic car chase ending in a crash. When the experience ended, guests removed their headsets to reveal a realistic smoking crash site – a curtain had been raised to reveal the surprise while they were "flying." They could then walk into the crash scene and into the Blade Runner world.

"We actually built a rain machine so you had to walk underneath gutters and roofing tiles," Marc said. "People were amazed when they took off the headset and could enter the Blade Runner world because the set design was immaculate in every detail. When the film's stars, Harrison Ford and Ryan Gosling, visited the installation, they thought it was the actual movie set."

As guests entered the crash scene, they moved forward into the soggy bar scene of the future, complete with 25 actors in costume ready to engage with them.

"We created a noodle bar so they could get a cup of noodles, like the classic movie," he said. "Johnny Walker was a sponsor of the film, so we had free Johnny Walker shots at the bar. The entire experience was built to be photographed and shared. We were also capturing the guest experience and sending our photos to the visitors at the end so they could post on social media.

"People who loved the film would wait in line for as long as six hours – and some of them did that twice! We truly created a marketing experience people were willing to pay for."

Giant Spoon activations aren't about gimmicks. The agency creates content and immersive experiences that reveal the brand's story in an organic, natural way.

"We highlight brand attributes, but in a way that makes people excited and engaged," Marc said. "When people are immersed in a quality story, they're more open to brand messages. In fact, if you're providing them with an amazing experience, they welcome it.

"We have this mantra for Giant Spoon: We're an ad agency that aspires to never make ads. That seems counter-intuitive, but we're convinced that businesses can't keep holding on to the old ways. We have to create strategies through the lens of the customer's values and culture. Lean into their moments. Lean into their trends. When you do that, they'll pay attention."

THE PRODUCT IS THE CONTENT

If you want to study a company that has mastered the Third Rebellion, look no further than Glossier. In fact, it was built on it.

Founder Emily Weiss began blogging about makeup in the early-morning hours before she reported for her job at *Vogue,* where she was a fashion assistant. Within a year, ad sales generated by her blog, *Into the Gloss,* allowed her to quit her day job. The blog had become a mecca for women curious about the latest skincare and makeup products, and it provided a forum for them to communicate with other beauty fans.

Feedback from her blog became Emily's R&D department. Based on the likes and dislikes of her readers, she developed her own beauty line, which launched in October 2014 to an eager audience of her 1.5 million hyper-engaged social media followers.

Glossier is one of the first major brands to be born out of social media, and it looks the part: Its modern, minimalist packaging is designed to look good in photographs. Every Glossier product arrives in a reusable, pink plastic pouch that doubles as an ideal Instagram backdrop.

While the company's competitors are being pummeled by Amazon, Glossier is thriving as a direct-to-consumer company that has raised more than $30 million in funding.

There were several key strategies behind Emily's success:

1. Human impressions

Before Emily built a business, she built her personal brand. She blogged for years and established a loyal audience who trusted her and her new company. Emily was the brand – a *human brand*.

Thirty-three percent of millennials (her key audience) rely mostly on the authenticity of personal blogs before they make a purchase, compared to fewer than 3 percent who prefer TV news, magazines, and books.[76]

Emily's plan was for customers to feel like the brand itself was a close friend – a friend who was a little older, maybe a little cooler, but never without a sense of humor or humility. "I wanted to create a brand whose sweatshirt you wanted to wear," she said. "I wanted a brand that didn't talk down to you, that treated you like a friend."[77]

2. User-generated content

More than 60 percent of millennials say that if a brand engages with them on social media, they're more likely to show loyalty to that brand.[78]

Nearly all of Glossier's marketing has been carried out by their own customers on social media. It's then curated and amplified by the home office.

The company sorts through thousands of hash-tagged photos each day to find their "real girl" models to feature on the Glossier social media feed. Fans work hard to promote the brand because they aspire to be a company model. This has turned the Glossier social media feed into a community of coolness – fun without pretense.

3. Meaning through shared values

Glossier is the makeup for people who reject the beauty queen ideal. But the brand's empowering attitude is also reflected in the company's content and marketing activities.

"Women are in the driver's seat," Emily said. "They are in charge of their routines, and they can find all the information they need from their friends or from other women in the world and online.

"There were very different value systems when other beauty brands were created in the '40s and '50s, and it had to do with glamour and a life of luxury. I think right now it's about power."[79]

4. Belonging as a path to innovation

Glossier was named one of the world's most innovative companies by *Fast Company* magazine. You wouldn't normally consider a beauty company as a wellspring of innovation, but Emily pulled it off with a little help from her friends.

In addition to skillfully turning social media feedback into an innovation pipeline, the company created a collaborative Slack channel for 100 of its top customers. Glossier receives more than 1,100 ideas each week, driving a steady flow of new product introductions.

5. Word-of-mouth marketing

Emily considers Glossier a content company: Each of her products is created as a word-of-mouth conversation starter. Every product and package is designed to be easily shared on social media. The products ship with a little strip of graffiti-doodle stickers inside, which customers plaster all over their stuff and post on social media.

"It's not about one person being the tastemaker," Emily said. "That's not how people are shopping anymore. Women are discovering beauty products through their friends, full stop."[80] Eighty percent of Glossier customers hear about the company through a peer recommendation.

The company shows off new items using common Instagram effects like "Boomerang" versus the traditional fashion shoots, to encourage the authentic user-generated look and feel. Glossier is also experimenting with experiential marketing and establishing "pop-up" beauty counters and restaurants in New York and San Francisco.

6. Reviews

Each Glossier product page is filled with customer reviews, and some of them are pretty honest, like this one: *"I wanted to like this a lot, but it's just ok. The smell is kind of nauseating."*

Encouraging reviews, even when they're negative, reflects the authenticity of the brand.

It's not unusual for Emily to participate on the comment boards, replying to her customers directly.

Emily doesn't see herself as a legendary fashion industry leader like Ralph Lauren or Estée Lauder. "A lot of our customers don't even know who I am," she said.

But she is someone who recognized the rebellion – technology was transforming the way beauty products were talked about and purchased. Emily built a great business because she's smart enough to know that the customers are in control, and she's wise enough to find ways to help them tell her story.

I hope you've enjoyed these case studies and feel inspired by these path-finding leaders. But simply hoping for a more human-centered marketing approach isn't going to drive any change. How do we make this new mindset come to life?

The biggest predictor of marketing success in the era of the rebellion has nothing to do with your budget or skillsets. You have to have the company culture to make the pivot. In fact, *your company culture is your marketing,* and I explain that in Chapter 11.

CHAPTER 11

THE QUANTUM LEAP

*"I have accepted fear as part of life –
specifically the fear of change ... I have gone
ahead despite the pounding in the heart that
says: turn back."*

—ERICA JONG

We've covered a lot of ground in our literary journey together,
but one problem remains. Now that you understand the
implications of the Third Rebellion and have a sense of what
you need to do about it, the battle ahead of you is convincing
your team and company leaders that change is needed.

Here are signs that you may be locked into a marketing
philosophy that won't work in the post-loyalty era:

- Adjusting your strategy and budget a little each year
  by "tweaking"
- Advertising much the same way you did three or five
  years ago
- Focusing on a "sales funnel" that isn't really there
- Locking into dysfunctional agency relationships

- Relying on press release distribution services to promote your ideas
- Prohibiting employees from posting about the company
- Relying on growth through TV or print advertising
- Posting any sort of stock social media content
- Feeling that you're in a constant state of falling behind
- Investing in marketing technology you don't understand
- Obsessing over dashboards instead of customers
- Abdicating your marketing leadership to a legal department
- ... or an IT department
- ... or anybody who has never been on Facebook or LinkedIn

In this chapter, I explore the organizational implications of the Third Rebellion. You know this is real. It's time to act. Now, what do you do about it?

QUANTUM LEADERSHIP

If you're leading a company or marketing organization, you're in the right position to make the changes needed to "get invited to the island." But if you're in the lower levels of an organization or acting in a consulting role, you might have some work to do.

There's no such thing as a grassroots cultural change. It has to come from the top. The person who controls the budget and the strategy also determines the company culture.

I witnessed one of the most dramatic examples of this ideal when I was in a company that was hurting too many employees. Our chairman, Paul O'Neill, decided to do something about it.

I was lucky to have spent much of my career at Alcoa. During my tenure there, Alcoa was a principled blue-chip company. Integrity mattered. Leadership mattered. I started at the company as a college intern, and I decided that I wanted to become a full-time employee if there was any chance that I could end up as smart and inspiring as the incredible leaders I met there.

Alcoa was a Fortune 100 company whose main line of business was mining, refining, and producing every type of aluminum product imaginable. The work environment in the mines and plants presented many opportunities to get hurt: massive machinery, molten metal, toxic chemicals, and fumes rising from "pots" heated to 1,400 degrees. Although the company operated in a professional and ethical way – adhering to every government safety standard – it was not unusual for people to get injured. And a couple times each year, somebody in the world of Alcoa was killed.

I'll never forget the sick feeling that swept through the company when we learned that an hourly employee, a young mother, had been crushed and killed by a piece of equipment at our Indiana plant. She had actually been on the plant safety committee and helped write the rule she violated in the accident. Every person in my office building walked around in stunned silence. I never thought I would attend a staff meeting where people cried and prayed.

When Paul O'Neill became chairman, he vowed this would never happen again – nobody would get hurt at this company. Frankly, most people thought he was irrational. There was just no way you could work in an industrial environment like Alcoa – where some of the plants were more than 100 years old – and not be at risk.

But Paul was determined and steadfast. He demanded a "quantum leap" change in our mentality. When people were getting injured, incremental improvement was unacceptable. He started every meeting with a discussion of safety. Every plant tour began with a challenge over safety. He even talked about safety on his quarterly calls with financial analysts.

And then something happened that changed the company forever.

At the annual shareholders meeting, a group of Catholic nuns from Mexico showed up in the front row of the auditorium. When it was time for the question and answer period, one of the nuns shyly raised a hand. She was acknowledged by the CEO and stood up to tell a story of how employees were being hurt in an Alcoa plant near Monterrey. She said she was attending the meeting in Pittsburgh to protest the work conditions. You could tell by the look on the chairman's face that he was gravely concerned, and he invited the nuns to meet privately with him after the public meeting.

As soon as it could be arranged, Paul boarded a company plane for Mexico to see for himself what was happening.

When he came back to the corporate office, he fired the group vice president responsible for the division and the working conditions at the plant. The person he fired was one of the most respected executives in the company and an obvious choice to lead it one day. He was five levels above the Monterrey plant manager. Nobody could believe this beloved leader, at that level of the company, had been fired over *safety*.

The message sent a tremor throughout the company. If it's possible to change a global corporate culture in one hour, it happened that day.

CULTURAL CHANGE STARTS AT THE TOP

What happened next seemed miraculous. New systems, training, and investments in safety helped the injury and incident rate plummet. Within a few years, the company's injury rate was statistically so low that it was safer to work at an Alcoa aluminum smelting plant than in a white-collar office job at IBM. The turnaround was so monumental that the company hosted professionals from other industries to teach them how to keep their people safe, too.

What Paul O'Neill realized was that transforming the culture was not just the right thing to do, it was the profitable thing to do. When a company cares deeply for employees, that culture naturally will extend to caring about processes, products, and customers. He showed through his leadership that we could do anything. If we could make a quantum leap in safety, why not in customer service, quality, and profitability?

We became a company of quantum leaps.

There's a powerful lesson here for all corporate change, and especially for the change needed in marketing, PR, and advertising. As I described early in the book, most marketers I know are asleep and don't even realize it. At Alcoa, we were asleep. We didn't know what our possibilities truly were. The culture was the culture ... and we lived with it. But it doesn't have to be that way. Principled, steadfast leadership can forge a new path.

Driving change in your organization might not begin with a word-of-mouth marketing effort or creating cool new customer experiences. It might mean getting your leadership onboard and helping them understand that the rebellion is inevitable, and that it's at your door.

PRACTICAL CULTURAL CHANGE

Adapting to this reality doesn't mean shifting a little. You need a quantum leap mentality. Here are considerations to drive this cultural change in your company:

- **Demonstrate change at the top:** Paul O'Neill didn't just set a goal and then go to lunch. He lived and breathed the goal. Anytime you met the man or saw him speak, there was no question that changing the culture was at the top of his agenda.

- **The right measure:** If you want to create a quantum leap in performance, you need to have a solid, unifying measurement that drives the right behaviors. The classic Jim Collins book, *Good to Great,* documents the importance of choosing the one true measure. In the Alcoa example, it was incident rate.

- **Peel back the curtains:** Customers want to believe in you, and in order to do that, they need to see who you really are. Author Mitch Joel put it well when he wrote the key to modern leadership is transparency: "Make visible that which is hidden: Data, business process, human resources, technology, sales, marketing, professional development, internal meetings, team performance, and the list goes on. There are countless areas where leaders can make significant advances, simply by making visible (to all) that which is hidden (to most)."

- **Submit to the truth:** The customers are our marketers. Surrendering to this insight will have profound consequences for your organization, your budget, and the people you're hiring to do the job. Accept the fact that two-thirds of your marketing is not your marketing. Now what are you going to do – starting today – to adjust to that new reality?

- **Take control:** I've railed against the misuse of technology. What's going on in your company? In stage one of the internet, marketing used technology to get people to bend. We wanted them to click, download, upload, view an ad. In the rebellion, we need to make the technology bend toward the consumer. Stop looking for the marketing easy button. Do your job and put technology in service of the customer.

- **Do something dramatic:** Paul O'Neill fired a friend, his second in command. It was a move calculated to send an earthquake throughout the organization. I'm not telling you to fire somebody, but you need to have zero tolerance for behaviors that are inconsistent with the changes that must be made.

THE ORGANIZATION

I've been thinking about what a human-centered marketing organization looks like. If you take the ideas from this book and build something from the ground up, what sort of talents do you need to have onboard?

One way to approach this question is to examine the groundbreaking companies I profile in the previous chapter: Fizz, Giant Spoon, Wren, Glossier, and Tony's Chocolonely. What I've realized is that their marketing teams are almost *entirely creative.*

These companies spend relatively little on traditional content production, SEO, or advertising. They focus their resources on creative new ways to connect to humans – through face-to-face interactions, entertaining experiences, intimate social media engagement, shareable moments, and by visiting people in their homes and workplaces, if necessary. They are relentlessly finding ways to help customers tell their stories.

It makes sense that to break through the noise, you have to generate something remarkable. Blog posts, SEO, and ads normally are not remarkable. So why keep doing it?

Simply put, the marketing department of the future will be populated by people with extraordinary ideas that your customers can love. (Once again, I'm NOT saying there's no place for ads, SEO, etc., but it's just not in the two-thirds, is it?)

In terms of organizational structure, I see several best practices across the companies I work with:

- **Functional alignment:** Most marketing teams are organized by product, brand, or region. But to be successful going forward, your team may need to be organized by functional expertise that can deliver integrated campaigns across all consumer touchpoints. This avoids creation of departments that outlive their usefulness.

- **IT-marketing integration:** There aren't many changes you can make to a website or eCommerce platform that don't impact user experience. Don't abdicate customer-facing decisions to the IT department. Marketing should have a seat at the IT table and infuse customer-first leadership into any public-facing technology decisions.

- **Meritocracy vs. hierarchy:** In traditional marketing organizations, job responsibilities and titles are hierarchical and unchanging. In the Third Rebellion world, everything is fluid. You need to reward people for creative contributions (that may be harder to measure) and the ability to shift into temporary roles as needed. When technology and consumer behavior patterns are changing so quickly, there may not be time to wait until the person assigned to the campaign gets around to a task.

What about the boss? Is there a still a role for the traditional chief marketing officer, or do you simply need a creative director?

Martin Lindstrom has some strong ideas about that: "The role of a traditional CMO is dead," he said "This job is over because CMOs have become number crunchers. They're looking at dashboards and reports and keeping track of all the new stuff happening in the media world, and so they always feel that they're behind. They're focusing on reacting, instead of the many amazing ideas that need to be launched right now.

"I see the new CMO as the glue between all divisions and functions in an organization. The marketing leader should be the person who is out among the customers finding new needs and opportunities, and then facilitating meetings between all the company departments, finding the potential synergies that could be brought to customers. The CMO should help people work together, always with the words of the customer in the middle of the game."

Jennifer Storms, CMO of NBC Sports Group,[81] agrees: "The role of a CMO is to go out, listen, and understand so they can represent the customer to the rest of the company."

She said there are three main functions to a successful CMO:

- **Educate:** Evangelize the customer across departments. Use the customer's language to explain what they want and what they value.

- **Analyze:** Strategy must be anchored in the data. Marketing has to own the consumer research and turn it into usable human insights.

- **Collaborate:** This is the most critical but often the most overlooked aspect of CMO success. Asking people to do things that are not necessarily in their best interests to serve the customer is hard to manage. The leader's role is to get teams to rally around the customer.

THE ROLE OF THE OUTSIDE AGENCY

I've been working with a brand manager at a huge pharmaceutical company who wants to implement some of the ideas from this book. But since she's locked into a global agency contract at her company, her progress has been confounded.

"I want to connect to consumers in new ways," she said. "I know what we're doing is a losing game. But every time I ask our agency for new approaches, it comes back as an ad. I'm so frustrated I'm ready to fire this agency even if it means that it costs my job!"

Nowhere is the alarm for change needed more than in the agency world. Our agency partners aren't just asleep – they're zombies who want to turn you into a zombie, too. The reason is simple. Agencies have been built over decades to pitch an idea, develop creative, execute, measure, and then bill enormous sums. They are so locked into their fossilized organizational structures that it's literally impossible for them to change. The cozy dance between corporate marketing leaders and their outside agencies must be disrupted to succeed.

"I'm pretty blunt here, but the advertising agency is a dying species," said Martin Lindstrom. "First, they're petrified of losing the clients, so they say 'yes' to everything, even when they know what they're doing is not working any more. Second, advertising agencies normally apply makeup to help old things look pretty. They don't actually change anything, yet many companies look to them for leadership."

Marketing budgets are rapidly moving away from traditional ad agencies to consulting firms like Accenture and Deloitte that are creating dramatic new customer experiences, disruptive strategies based on data-based insights, frictionless eCommerce, and value personalized to individual needs.[82]

Agencies can still provide the essential creative fuel needed to market successfully in the Third Rebellion, but it has to be in service of the reality of the world as it is today, which means a focus on helping the customers do the marketing for us.

MEASUREMENT

Writing a book is sort of like getting a new master's degree. For two years, I'm reading, researching, and writing about what's here and what's next. And one thing I've realized from all this studying is that measurement – or the lack of it – will be a significant hurdle to winning in the world of the Third Rebellion.

Many forms of marketing currently in our control can be measured, especially the digital variety. The type of marketing I propose in this book may be very difficult to connect to conversions and sales – impossible, in some cases. That two-thirds of marketing that's out of our control – the consumer content, the reviews, the word-of-mouth conversations – is vitally important, but it doesn't fit neatly into the current marketing dashboard.

- How do you measure your success in helping people belong?
- What are the short-term measures of progress in a word-of-mouth marketing program?
- How does a small company quantify the long-term impact of taking a stand and aligning with customer values?
- How do you measure the value of experiential marketing like the *Blade Runner* example in Chapter 10?

Of course, you can measure just about anything with enough creativity and diligence, but it's not easy, and marketers and their bosses tend to migrate toward the easy, the familiar, the neat data entry for the departmental monthly report.

"When people can't measure, they just hold onto the old ways," observed Marc Simons of Giant Spoon. "Even the best leaders get stopped in their tracks on the measurement question. They're well-read. They understand the pulse of culture. They know they need to do better. But moving to a culture of marketing innovation takes courage. You need an enlightened leader to drive this sort of change and abandon traditional measures.

"You can keep up with the accelerating pace of culture, or you can measure. You probably can't do both."

I agree with this statement ... and I hate this statement. It makes me feel decidedly un-businesslike to advocate anything we can't measure. The famous American author Peter Drucker is bellowing in my head: "If you can't measure it, you can't manage it!"

According to analytics expert Julie Ferrara at The University of Tennessee, marketers will need to think beyond the current marketing dashboard to drive quantum change in their organizations.

"Today's measures are based on historical performance," she said. "When you experiment with word-of-mouth, influencer marketing, and other new ideas, there's no benchmark for assessment, so naturally that's regarded as an organizational risk.

"But companies should allocate part of their marketing budget to experimenting with new methods and take a calculated risk based on expected outcomes. You have to be okay not having a trend line to rely on. Instead, you should set goals for an event or activation and then conduct a post-mortem – did we reach our goals? You can then begin a journey of continuous learning and process improvement that will eventually lead to more obvious and measurable business benefits.

"You also have to remove emotion from the process. It's okay to miss goals, iterate, and improve, but you also need to set objectives and follow them, so you know when it's time to quit and move on to something else."

Author Seth Godin writes in his book, *This Is Marketing*, that measurement anxiety is the new norm:

"Direct marketing is action oriented. And it is measured.

"Brand marketing is culturally oriented. And it can't be measured.

"The approach here is as simple as it is difficult. If you're buying direct marketing ads, measure everything. Compute how much it costs you to earn attention, to get a click, to turn that attention into an order. Direct marketing is action marketing, and if you're not able to measure it, it doesn't count.

"If you're doing brand marketing, be patient. Refuse to measure. Engage with the culture. Focus, by all means, but mostly be consistent and patient."

Your challenge is to come alongside your customers, even if you can't pin down the ROI right away. Or put another way, what will be the cost to you if you *don't change* your marketing approach ... and your competitors do?

PROCUREMENT

Another obstacle related to measurement is the procurement process. If it's difficult to measure these new marketing tactics, how do you create a specification for them?

"There are clients still treating marketing like we're in the '80s or the '90s," said Marc Simons. "Procurement departments only know a certain toolset, and they stick with it. If they haven't kept up with the new voices in marketing and the new technology, they don't even know what to ask for.

"Procurement professionals are trained to drill down to the lowest common denominator. Ultimately, they want to define the performance of a campaign. How many sales? How many leads? They're trying to compare new marketing to what has worked in the past, and it's impossible to do that."

YOUR CULTURE IS YOUR MARKETING

When I was doing research for this book, I asked my friends for examples of companies that made their customers feel like they belong. A company called Wistia kept coming up in these conversations. People were *raving* about this company like I would rave about the Pittsburgh Steelers. Real fans.

So I checked them out. Wistia offers a package of tools so businesses can produce, manage, and store their video content. But this is what got my attention: The company website proclaims that Wistia is 81 people and one dog working to make business more human.

Hello, Wistia. You have my attention.

When I interviewed the company's founder and CEO, Chris Savage, I intended to write a case study for the "belonging" chapter. But I soon realized that Chris is exactly the kind of leader who is not only adapting to the Third Rebellion, he is leading it, with a quantum leap.

I decided to publish the interview in its entirety because it offers a valuable lesson in marketing leadership and a company built on human impressions.

MARK: Chris, you've mentioned in other interviews that you feel your greatest achievement is establishing an effective corporate culture. Was it intentional for this culture to extend to the way you connect to customers?

CHRIS: No, I can't say it was intentional at first. When we started out, our website was kind of fun, but we didn't have any deliberate marketing program. We were messing around in our office and just shot a video that was "behind the scenes" of what it was like to work here. No voice-over or anything – just shots of the team working to music. And the little video made it to *Hacker News,* and it went viral. People were talking about how cool and interesting Wistia was.

I thought we were on to something, so we tried more of that kind of open video. We did it for our own enjoyment – it was essentially something we could send to our parents! The irony is, these simple videos were never intended to attract customers. We weren't selling a thing. And two weeks later ... we had a bunch of new customers!

It was this interesting moment because we had been talking about our product *a lot* and we weren't moving very fast. And then we *stopped* talking about our product and just showed who we are, and we had new customers coming to us every day.

I learned that *our company culture is our marketing.* I began to realize that if I screw up the culture of this company, it will directly impact our ability to market ourselves. Customers are making an emotional connection to the people in our videos, even more than to the product itself.

I'm not saying we're perfect. We went through a time of focusing on the wrong things that hurt us all around. But once I got clear on our culture, things started to click because the culture is strategy, right? If you're not able to be honest and transparent internally, you're not going to achieve that with customers, either.

The success comes from creating a culture that enables storytelling, connections, and community. It goes back to all those things that mattered to us before the internet.

Was there an experience or event that made you realize that you had more than customers? You had fans who were buying into your company and your culture?

Six years ago, we thought it would be fun to put on an event for our customers and walk them through what we had been learning. We put something out on Twitter – announced that we were having a meet-up on this certain Saturday. And we'd never put on an event before, we had no idea how many people were going to come. We had a very small following on social media. So, we thought five people will come to this thing. And 60 people showed up, and some of them had driven a long distance from other states.

And they said, "I'm so excited to talk with your team. You're on to something new, you're on to something different, this company feels really good." It was a remarkable moment. I sensed they were rooting for us. It was something stronger than simply a customer relationship.

Some people cheer for sports teams. And some people cheer for start-ups. I suppose we're the sports team for nerds! Our customers were paying attention to who was on our team, what moves we were making. They started wearing our shirts and displaying our stickers, just like you would for a favorite sports team. And most important, they were telling their friends about us.

Most of our customers come through referrals, and the referrals come from word of mouth – people who are talking about the stories of the brand and the cool new things we do.

The average lifetime of our customer is about five years right now, which is a very long time for a typical small business. So the customer loyalty from these connections is showing up on the bottom line.

What's the difference between being a leader of a company that has customers versus leading a company that has a dedicated community of fans?

Having a relationship with customers is transactional. Having a relationship with fans is ongoing. Fans want to be part of what you do – they want to know the news before it happens and you have to respond to that. "Customers" in the traditional sense are people who shop around and don't really care about your team and culture.

The fans who root for you want to see behind the scenes, they want to be involved. That's a very powerful need that you have to respect. Serving a true community means constantly investing in that long-term relationship.

So, it's above and beyond just communicating with them. How are customers actually *involved* in your company?

That's a great question. The biggest thing we do is involve our top customers in our product planning. As we're trying to figure out what's next, we have processes in place to talk to customers and discover the big problems we can solve. As we get closer to solutions, we have testing groups who are willing to use stuff that might not work. The customers dictate the roadmap. They are pretty much in control of our development process.

We also host events where we bring the community together in person and online. We're out there talking to customers every day. We have thousands of people who we talk to on a monthly basis – probably 6,000 to 10,000, depending on the month.

We did something recently called Video Marketing Week – all online – and we had 8,500 people sign up. And next we've planned Couch Con, which is designed to be a conference with 20 different speakers that you can join from your couch. We're always thinking of creative new ways to connect and involve our customers.

The customer experience even dictates how the company is structured. We're always asking, "Do we have the right structure to match what our customers want?" We're not afraid to adjust.

How do you manage those thousands of conversations? You're a sizable company now and I can see how you can risk disappointing people if a fan gets lost as the company gets bigger.

That's a very important concern for us. We have several processes in place to make sure nothing slips through the cracks.

One of the ways we capture feedback and ideas is through online forums. We pay for our customers to have a Slack membership so they can access different areas of our company. We have a "general room" that has 2,300 people active online on a daily basis. And then there are areas for general advice, marketing advice, sales advice, production advice, and other questions. People can also create their own channels around specific events and products. We keep an eye on things, but to a large degree, this is a community that is helping each other. That was the dream – working as an integrated and organic team with our customers.

The other advantage to this system is that the history of all these engagements doesn't disappear like it might in a customer visit. We're spending a lot of money on this system, but it's worth it just to make sure these conversations are fruitful and customers see the evidence that we're listening, we're acting, we're transparent.

What matters to me is that Wistia is a company our customers are invested in, that they believe in, that they want to learn from, that they cheer for.

*****

I hope that I will be an author that people will cheer for! That seems like a very relevant goal.

The powerful lesson in the Wistia case study is that if you truly connect in a personal and human way, your "marketing" can end. If you're delivering a product that solves a problem, then the human-centered culture of your company and organic customer connection drives demand and sales.

Let's head into our last chapter together and look forward. Could there be a Fourth Rebellion?

CHAPTER 12

THE FOURTH REBELLION

"To say goodbye is to die a little."
—RAYMOND CHANDLER

The end of lies.

The end of secrets.

The end of control.

Is this the final rebellion, or can we peer far enough into the future to predict what the next generation of marketers will face?

Today, I believe that establishing the emotional connection of branding is more important than ever, but we're moving into an era where even that marketing truth becomes obsolete. Eventually companies will collect and collate personal information about us down to the specifics of our DNA. We'll be marketed to on a molecular level.

In an essay entitled "The End of Advertising," Alexander Nethercutt writes:

> *The perfection of data will eventually give rise to a world in which every consumer can be paired with goods that meet his or her biological, rather than consumptive, tendencies. This world will be devoid of branding, because in a world that relies on perfect information, there will be no need for branded trust. The cheaper of two identical goods will always be purchased, as opposed to what happens now – a consumer pays more for Motrin (the brand), than ibuprofen (the drug), even though they're the same thing.*

> *Once perfect information becomes a reality, there won't be just a few over-the-counter meds to alleviate pain; there will be hundreds, or even thousands, depending on the specific needs of the niche markets. The purpose of marketing in this world will be to pair niche consumers, whose needs were never profitable enough to be met, with niche products, whose production was never profitable enough to be realized.*

> *Advertising as we've always known it – large-scale campaigns predicated on instilling subconscious intuition in consumers – will die. What will rise from its ashes will be unlike anything we've seen before. Algorithms buried within the walls of companies like Google and Facebook and Amazon will present us with our ideal options for everything, because they will know us best.*

In *Marketing Rebellion,* I've concluded that the customer is now the marketer. In the future, the customer could also become *the market* – a market of one.

I don't completely subscribe to Alexander's dystopian view because I think a certain part of us will always be irrational and reach for the Motrin anyway.

But undeniably, the internet hive mind already knows more about us than we know about ourselves. Perhaps the only thing preventing the fourth rebellion is that we haven't awakened to that reality yet. When we realize that we're better served by allowing algorithms to take care of our everyday decisions, will the response simply be tired resignation, or will the next rebellion be about the right to exert our imperfect free will?

The speed of change makes the future murky. But there's one certainty: Whatever the battle, the consumers will eventually win, as they always have.

And we *must* follow their lead.

Some businesses will never get it. Others will continue to resist. But the human-centered marketing movement *will* happen. I am sure of this because Dr. Robert Cialdini told me so.

I had the honor of interviewing Dr. Cialdini for a previous book I published. He's an academic hero of mine and the author of several *New York Times* best-selling books including *Influence at Work* and *Pre-suasion.*

At the end of our interview, I asked, "Dr. Cialdini, in this very noisy, overwhelming world, what can anybody do to stand out?"

Without hesitation, he said just three words: "Be. More. Human."

In a world dominated by algorithmic efficiency, the human touch creates meaning, emotion, and impact. The more I learn about our tumultuous business world, the more I dwell on our problems and challenges, the more I am certain Dr. Cialdini is right.

Be more human.

No matter what happens next, if we use that as our constant guide and filter, we'll be okay.

The most human company wins.

*****

This is the end of *Marketing Rebellion* the book, but Marketing Rebellion the movement is just beginning. Best wishes on your journey toward more human-centered marketing. Thank you so much for spending this time with me and my book – I'll never take you and your support for granted. Stay in touch, won't you?

Mark Schaefer

APPENDIX

THE CREATIVE PROCESS BEHIND THE BOOK

In 1545, Jacopo da Pontormo scored a major commission from the powerful Medici family to paint the main chapel of Florence's Basilica of San Lorenzo. A contemporary of masters like Michelangelo, Pontormo was a distinguished but aging artist who was eager to secure his legacy.

Pontormo knew he needed to make the frescoes the crowning achievement of his career, so he sealed off the entire chapel. He built walls and hung blinds so that nobody could steal his ideas or sneak an early peek. He spent 11 years holed up this way, painting Christ on Judgment Day, Noah's ark, and the Creation of the World.

The old artist died before his work was completed, and none of it survives. But a Renaissance writer visited the site soon after the painter's death. He reported a confused composition and a disturbing lack of continuity, scenes that ran into each other every which way. The frescoes were visual representations of the effects of isolation on the human mind.

I don't isolate myself in the dramatic fashion of Pontormo, but I do spend a lot of my writing time alone in my office in the woods. It's a conundrum. I need the isolation to concentrate, but I miss the human interactions that would make the book richer and more complete.

In the middle of the research for this book, an event occurred that changed the way I will write forever.

At the annual SXSW conference in Austin, I had the honor to meet and interview Walter Isaacson, the acclaimed author of biographies on Steve Jobs, Albert Einstein, and others. But we spent most of our time together discussing the nature of genius and his new book on Leonardo da Vinci, who also lived in the time of Pontormo.

Leonardo was arguably the most creative human being who ever lived, a magical genius who was endlessly curious. What struck me was how many of his ideas were collaborative. Even his most famous illustration, "Vitruvian Man," was inspired by Vitruvius, a Roman author, architect, and civil engineer who lived centuries before Leonardo's time.

Leonardo was a beloved man and always surrounded by friends. One day, his friend Francesco showed him a sketch of a man in a circle, based on the detailed descriptions from a Vitruvian book. Part of the Renaissance movement was rediscovering ancient ideas and reframing them in modern terms, and Francesco was excited by his revelation. It spurred Leonardo to consider the dimensions of a human being in mathematical terms.

Another friend, Giacomo Andrea, scribbled some interpretations of the Vitruvian idea and showed Leonardo how the human figure could be circumscribed in a circle.

Leonardo was mesmerized by the idea and inspired to find his own manuscript of Vitruvius' ancient work. Leonardo developed his own drawing from those ideas, and in both scientific precision and artistic beauty, his illustration is in an entirely different realm than the work of his predecessors.

Some believe the famous work could even be a self-portrait. And, it was a collaboration. The now-famous drawing was built upon an ancient idea that inspired a scribbled drawing by a friend that led to a discussion. Yes, Leonardo delivered something exquisite and unique, but it only could have happened with the help of others. The iconic drawing was a combination of ideas from four different people.

As I read about this, and many other examples of Leonardo's collaborations, I had an awakening about my own creative process. My previous books had largely been a lonely and isolated process. Of course I did research and interviews. But in terms of framing the book, it was all taking place by myself ... in a big chair, in a quiet office, in total isolation. For this book, I was inspired by Leonardo and set upon a plan to speak to and, in most cases, meet with thought leaders who could help forge the main ideas of the book.

The impact of these in-depth conversations was profound. The ideas of my brilliant friends are woven into the book like the mesh of a fine tapestry. Stand back to view the cloth, and the individual threads combine to make something sturdy and beautiful. Sometimes my friends are mentioned by name and sometimes their whispers are behind the words, but all had a hand in the creative process. Here is my DaVinci Team:

Chad Parizman, Director, Digital Marketing, Pfizer

Megan Conley, CEO and founder of Social Tribe

Melyssa Banda, VP Channel Marketing,
Seagate Technologies

Fabio Tambosi, Brand Marketing Director, Adidas

Dane Hartzell, Digital Marketing Director, Honeywell

Jack Silverman, Marketing Director, Bolin Marketing

Dr. Karen Freberg, Professor at University of Louisville

Dorothéa Bozicolona-Volpe, Marketing and branding
consultant

Dr. Joseph Haas, Psychologist

Jess Bahr, Engineer, Marketing consultant

Hayut Yogev, Consultant to Israeli start-ups

Ann Handley, founder of Marketing Profs

Steve Rayson, Entrepreneur and founder of BuzzSumo

Bernadette Jiwa, Author and marketing consultant

Kristian Strøbech, Journalist, educator, and consultant

Melissa Wilson, CEO, Networlding

Jeremy Floyd, CMO, attorney, and entrepreneur

Jay Acunzo, Entrepreneur

Mitch Joel, Entrepreneur, author, and former President
of Mirum

Arthur Carmichael, Producer, Scripps Networks

Jill Stone, Artist

Kitty Kilian, Teacher of writing and journalism

Martin Lindstrom, Branding expert and consultant

Ted Wright, Word-of-mouth marketing expert and entrepreneur

Amit Panchal, Director of Competitive Strategy, Microsoft

Keith Reynold Jennings, VP of Community Impact, Jackson Healthcare

Olga Andrienko, Head of Global Marketing, SEMrush

Julie Ferrara, University of Tennessee

I am indebted to each and every one of these thought leaders for their generous insights and support. I hope you found our work to be memorable.

ACKNOWLEDGEMENTS

This book has been an incredible work of love, created over more than two years through the help of a wonderful team of people.

Keith Reynold Jennings first introduced himself to me as a fan of my book *KNOWN* and since then we've become friends and business philosophy soul mates. Keith is Vice President of Community Impact of Atlanta's Jackson Healthcare and added his wisdom while reviewing early drafts of my book.

Kitty Kilian is a Holland-based writing authority. She is my drill sergeant, ruthlessly questioning details in my drafts and assuring *Marketing Rebellion* was meaningful to a diverse and international audience.

A big message in my book is the importance of creating a local, artisanal marketing approach. I wanted that "hand-crafted" look for my book and hired a Knoxville-based illustrator, Paris Woodhull, to oversee the look and feel of the book. She delivered.

Mandy Edwards was indispensable in her editorial support throughout this process and helped deliver the vital research and fact-checking to make the stories of *Marketing Rebellion* complete, accurate, and entertaining.

Kelly Exeter did the beautiful interior layout and Elizabeth Rea is my long-time editor who helps make my words sing.

Last but not least, I owe so much to my wife Rebecca whose patient encouragement and wise counsel soothed me throughout the excruciating process of writing a book.

All my gifts come from God. My prayer is that this book has glorified Him in some small way.

ABOUT THE AUTHOR

Mark W. Schaefer is a globally-recognized speaker, educator, business consultant, and author who blogs at {grow} — one of the top marketing blogs of the world.

Mark has worked in global sales, PR, and marketing positions for more than 30 years and now provides consulting services as Executive Director of U.S.-based Schaefer Marketing Solutions. He specializes in marketing training and clients include both start-ups and global brands such as Dell, Johnson & Johnson, Adidas, and the U.S. Air Force.

Mark has advanced degrees in marketing and organizational development and is a faculty member of the graduate studies program at Rutgers University. A career highlight was studying under Peter Drucker while studying for his MBA.

He is the author of six other best-selling books, *The Tao of Twitter, Social Media Explained, Return On Influence, Born to Blog, The Content Code,* and *KNOWN*. His Marketing

Companion podcast is among the top 1 percent of business shows on iTunes.

Mark is among the world's most recognized marketing authorities and has been a keynote speaker at many conferences around the world including Social Media Week London, National Economic Development Association, the Institute for International and European Affairs, and Word of Mouth Marketing Summit Tokyo.

You can stay connected and follow along with Mark at www.BusinessesGROW.com and by following his adventures on Twitter: @markwschaefer

KEEP LEARNING ABOUT MARKETING REBELLION

Please visit our website www.businessesGROW.com/rebellion to find:

- A free workbook and bonus materials
- New case studies and posts
- A downloadable word-of-mouth marketing workbook
- A hand-illustrated coloring book featuring ideas from the book
- Special offers for educators
- Information about bulk book sales

ENDNOTES

CHAPTER 1 - THE END OF CONTROL

1 Much of this section was inspired by the excellent book "The Attention Merchants: The Epic Scramble to Get Inside our Heads" by Tim Wu, published by Alfred A. Knopf, 2016

2 "The consumer decision journey," by David Court, Dave Elzinga, Susan Mulder, and Ole Jørgen Vetvik, McKinsey & Company Insights

3 "Ten years on the consumer decision journey: Where are we today?" on McKinsey blog Nov. 17, 2017

CHAPTER 2 - ALL THINGS HUMAN

4 "The Relevancy Gap: Businesses Believe Marketing Communications Are Effective; Consumers Disagree" by Tom Farrell on martechseries.com

5 "Do Brands Follow Through on Their Promises? Many Are Skeptical" Commentary and charts on Marketing Charts October 2018

6 "MarTech's Evolving More Rapily than Marketer's Use of It" by Marketing Charts July 30, 2018

7 2017 Alphabet annual Founder's Letter

8   Nielsen data from "Large B2C Brands Are Struggling to Optimize Their Marketing Budgets" on Marketing Charts blog August 01, 2018

9   "Jeff Bezos Says This 1 Surprising Strategy Is the Secret to His Remarkable Success," By Peter Economy INC magazine Jan 2018

CHAPTER 3 – LOVE AND THE END OF LOYALTY

10   "The new battleground for marketing-led growth" McKinsey Quarterly Journal Feb 2017 by David Court, Dave Elzinga, Bo Finneman, and Jesko Perrey

11   "What's Love Got to do With It?" By Isabelle Coates, WGSN blog, July 06, 2018

12   "Survey: 32 percent of consumers say brands are delivering less on promises," by Adrianne Pasquarelli, Ad Age Oct 09, 2018

13   "Your Guide to Generation Z" By Elizabeth Segran, Fast Company Magazine, April 18, 2016

14   Source for the section on Macy's comes from "Employers Are Looking for 'Influencers' Within Their Own Ranks" by Amy Merrick, The Atlantic, Sept. 27, 2018

15   McKinsey, ibid

16   Google partnered with Verto Analytics to analyze the consumer opt-in Verto Smart Cross-Device Audience Measurement Panel for click-stream data of n=2,989 individuals over a period of six months.

CHAPTER 4 – BELONGING: THE GREATEST HUMAN NEED

17   "Genes are nice but joy is better" By Liz Mineo, Harvard Gazette, April 11, 2017

18 "Young people may be the loneliest of all" by Dalmeet Singh Chawla" on Medium, Oct. 1, 2018

19 "The Blindness of Social Wealth" By David Brooks, The New York Times, April 16, 2018

20 "No employee is an island: Workplace loneliness and job performance" by Ozcelik and Barsade, Academy of Management Journal, Feb. 6, 2018

21 "U.K. Appoints a Minister for Loneliness" By Ceylan Yeginsu, The New York Times, Jan. 17, 2018

22 The source material for the Pepsi case study comes from the book "The Attention Merchants: The Epic Scramble to Get Inside our Heads," by Tim Wu, published by Alfred A. Knopf, 2016

23 "How 2 Brothers Turned a $300 Cooler Into a $450 Million Cult Brand" by Bill Saporito, INC magazine online edition

24 Some of these tips from Lululemon come from the article "How Lululemon Uses Ambassadors to Foster Customer Engagement" by Laura Hill, Well To Do, July 13, 2017

25 "4 Tactics Lululemon Uses to Leverage Word-of-Mouth for their Brand" by Samuel Hum ReferralCandy Blog, June 30, 2015

26 Some of these foundational ideas are based on research found in "Getting Brand Communities Right" by Susan Fournier and Lara Lee; Harvard Business Review, April 2009

27 "Advertising is dead and other thoughts from Faith Popcorn," by John Wolfe, Media Post, March 16, 2018

28 Molly Battin quotes were from a live event, Brand Marketing Summit, October, 2018

CHAPTER 5 - SELF-INTEREST & THE ARTISANAL BRAND

29 "The Localist Revolution" by David Brooks, The New York Times, July 19, 2018

30 "Why trust and transparency are crucial components of brand success" by Lynette Saunders, eConsultancy, April 2018

31 http://adage.com/article/podcasts/mastercard-marketer-existential-threat-faces-cmos/313766/

32 Source: "Nintendo's New DIY Toys Are Mind-Bendingly Imaginative" by Harry McCracken, Fast Company, April 13, 2018

33 Source: "Why this clothing startup wants you to know thy T-shirt maker" by Elizabeth Segran, Fast Company, July 10, 2018

34 Source: "Why Companies Need a New Digital Playbook to Succeed in the Digital Age" by Peter Weill and Stephanie Woerner, MIT Sloan Management Review, June 2018

CHAPTER 6 - VALUES-BASED MARKETING AND THE SEARCH FOR MEANING

35 From the book "Story Driven: You don't need to compete when you know who you are," by Bernadette Jiwa

36 "9 Out of 10 People Are Willing to Earn Less Money to Do More-Meaningful Work" by Achor, Reece, Kellerman, and Robichaux, Harvard Business Review, November 6, 2018

37 "Advertising is dead and other thoughts from Faith Popcorn" by John Wolfe, Media Post, March 16, 2018

38 Some information about American Eagle for this case study came from "How gun control and gay rights became key to selling jeans" by Elizabeth Segran, Fast Company, July 30, 2018

39 Three myths about what customers want" by Karen Freeman, Patrick Spenner and Anna Bird, Harvard Business Review, May 23, 2012

40 "Consumers Believe Brands Can Help Solve Societal Ills" by Suzanne Vranica, Wall Street Journal, October 02, 2018

41 Source of BlackRock information: "BlackRock's Message: Contribute to Society, or Risk Losing Our Support" by Andrew Ross Sorkin, The New York Times, January 15, 2018

42 Quote from live event Brand Marketing Conference, October 2018

43 "Report: CEOs taking a stand online can boost reputation and sales" by Beki Winchel, PR Daily, September 7, 2018

44 This is from a 2018 study that can be found at CMOstudy.org.

45 Source for this section: "As Millennials Demand More Meaning, Older Brands Are Not Aging Well" by Sebastian Buck, Fast Company, October 5, 2017

46 Many thanks to Keith Reynold Jennings for contributing this HBR insight.

47 Quote from Kindle version of the book "Hit Refresh" by Satya Nadella, Greg Shaw and Jill Tracie Nichols

CHAPTER 7 - "RESPECT ME": A CALL FOR CONSENSUAL MARKETING

48 "The most hated online advertising techniques" by Therese Fessenden, Nielsen Norman Group, June 4, 2017

49 "Do brands have enough MarTech now?" Marketing Charts, October 10, 2018

50 Source of Mr. Rothenberg's quotes are "Tackling the Internet's Central Villain: The Advertising Business" by Farhad Manjoo, The New York Times, February 1, 2018

51 "The new consumer decision journey" by David Edelman and Marc Singer, McKinsey.com, October 2015

52 The New Tech Manifesto is an open, crowd-sourced document. You can contribute to the effort, too by visiting bit.ly/datafesto

53 "Why trust & transparency are crucial components of brand success" by Lynette Saunders, eConsultancy blog April 05, 2018

CHAPTER 9 - YOUR CUSTOMERS ARE YOUR MARKETERS

54 "Connecting Process to Customer: Take the Customer Journey" by Bruce Robertson, Gartner.com, May 3, 2017

55 Data from "Freemium conversion rate: Why Spotify destroys Dropbox" by Brandon Brindall, process.st, June 28, 2018

56 Quote and statistics from "Denver: The WSJ Airport Rankings' Rocky Mountain High-Scorer" by Scott McCartney, Wall Street Journal, November 14, 2018

57 "User Generated Content is Transforming B2C Marketing" by Matthew Hutchinson, Salesforce Marketing blog, February 17, 2016

58 "11 Ways To Engage Customers In Your Marketing Strategy" Forbes Communication Council, June 12, 2018

59 "The science behind why people follow the crowd" by Rob Henderson, Psychology Today, May 24, 2017

60 "New Study Finds that 19 Percent of Sales Are Driven by Consumer Conversations Taking Place Offline and Online" on Engagement Labs blog, November 27, 2017

61 "Aliza Freud on Influencer Marketing" by Matthew Quint, Columbia Business School Ideas and Insights, February 20, 2017

62 "Glossier is building a multimillion-dollar millennial empire with Slack, Instagram and selfies" by Jenni Avins, Quartz, December 1, 2016

63 "Social Objects: Everything you wanted to know" by Hugh Macleod, Gaping Void blog, July 24, 2017

64 "What really makes customers buy a product" by Hugh N. Wilson, Emma K. Macdonald, Shane Baxendale, Harvard Business Review, November 9, 2015

65 Case study comes from "The Power of Moments" by Chip and Dan Heath

66 "How Customers Come to Think of a Product as an Extension of Themselves" by Colleen P. Kirk, Harvard Business Review, September 17, 2018

67 "How 'normal people' are taking over the product review" by Ken Wheaton, Think With Google Blog, April 2018

68 Source: YouTube Data, U.S., Classification "travel diary and vlog" videos were based on public data such as headlines, tags, etc., and may not account for every such video available on YouTube, Jan. - June 2015 and 2017.

69 "Influence Marketing Sways Youth Who Engage With It" By Marketing Charts, April 9, 2018

70 "The Right Way to Market to Millennials" by Jay I. Sinha and Thomas T. Fung, MIT Sloan Management Review, April 24, 2018

71 Disclosure: I have been considered an influencer for Dell in the past and currently host the company's "Luminaries" podcast.

72 "Three Short-Term Trends from The Latest CMO Survey" from Marketing Charts, September 18, 2018

73 "It's time to put an end to the era of lazy marketing" by Mark Schaefer, {grow} blog, October 17, 2017

74 Quote from "Six Content Ideas Every Marketer Should Steal From IBM" by Marcia Riefer Johston, Content Marketing Institute, January 14, 2016

CHAPTER 10 – THE PATHFINDERS

75 "Wren's Melissa Coker on how that Viral 'First Kiss' Video Went Down" by Dhani Mau, Fashionista, March 11, 2014

76 "Ten new findings about the millennial consumer" by Dan Schwabel, Forbes, January 15, 2015

77 "How the founder of Glossier created a beauty line with a cult following" by Ahiza Garcia, CNN Business, October 11, 2017

78 Ibid Schwabel

79 Quote from "How fast can a beauty blogger become the millennials' Estée Lauder? About three years" by Amy Larocca, The Cut

80 Ibid Larocca

CHAPTER 11 – THE QUANTUM LEAP

81 Quotes from live presentation at Brand Marketing Summit 2018.

82 "Tech consultants are the new Mad Men" by Stephen Wilmot, The Wall Street Journal, November 9, 2018

INDEX

Made in the USA
San Bernardino, CA
25 November 2019